CONFESSIONS
OF A BASEBALL CARD ADDICT

Tanner Jones

ISBN: 9781731198464

www.TanManBaseballFan.com
www.CansecoCollector.com
www.CustomCutsOnline.com

The stories contained in this book are not from any specific game, event, or season.

TABLE OF CONTENTS

In Memory of my Dad
Duane Clark Jones

"Papa Bear"
8/12/54 – 10/9/18

PROLOGUE

I feel like I've always been a much better communicator on paper than by using my voice. There is just something about writing that piques my creative side. With the right words, you can make someone feel good about themselves and motivate them to do great things.

With the right words, you can create a rich and vibrant landscape - you can use your reader's brain to paint your memory as if it were their own! As you continue reading this book, I want you to be able to picture yourself in my shoes at the baseball card show, taking in the sounds of the people's voices overlapping as they make deals on cards. I want your eyes to dilate when you read about how bright the 1991 Fleer borders were and I want your memory to smell 1992 Stadium Club again. I want you to recall how cringe-worthy it was to find that the best card in the pack was off-center, and I want you to feel the excitement of what it was like to be able to open an entire box of baseball cards all by yourself.

Cardboard runs in my veins, and if you are reading this, there is a good chance it does with you, too. I can recall the earliest memories of my life because of baseball cards, and it is because of baseball cards that I have learned many valuable life lessons. God has blessed me with an incredible journey in this hobby, and I'm very thankful that you have chosen to read about it! I hope you love reading this book as much as I loved writing it. So, with all that said, let's jump right in. My name is Tanner Jones. I am a baseball card addict, and this is my story.

To Err is Human;
To Collect, Divine

Did You Know?

Ever wonder why Topps gum isn't soft? The gum
was made hard intentionally, so it could be
mechanically inserted into packs without buckling.

Do you remember the first time you were hooked on baseball cards? For me, it was in California as a child in the 1980s. Growing up, California was a hotbed for baseball. You had the California Angels (or was it the LA Angels? The Angels of Anaheim? I give up!), Los Angeles Dodgers, San Francisco Giants, San Diego Padres and my favorite team, the Oakland Athletics.

I was fairly oblivious to baseball at an early age, and it certainly wasn't in my DNA. As a matter of fact, my dad told my mom when I first got into baseball, that he didn't even like the sport. Mom leaked that information to me a few years into my obsession. At first, it sounded like treason to say such a thing, but she was merely trying to make a point that he was trying to take an interest in what I liked to have a closer relationship with me.

At around the age of nine, my obsessive attention was focused almost entirely on baseball. I cannot quite pinpoint the exact time or reason this happened, but it did. Perhaps I saw a colorful display of packs in the aisle at Target. Maybe it was all the other kids around me talking about their favorite baseball players. Or perhaps it was the Mother's Cookies in the pantry that came with a baseball card. Back then, everything came with a baseball card - I miss those days! All I know is when the baseball card bug bit me, it bit me hard.

THE BEST TRADE I NEVER MADE

Before we dive into the genesis of my collecting, let's rewind a couple of years. My family and I were visiting some friends a few hours away, and their son Charlie wanted to go to the baseball card shop. At about seven years old, I confess I didn't know what a card shop was. I recall that it was quite dark, and cramped. Fluorescent lights flickered and reflected off of the glass cases that displayed these strange pieces of cardboard worth a lot of money for reasons that were beyond me.

Confessions of a Baseball Card Addict

Charlie wanted a pack of baseball cards, and I figured I would ask for one too. Our parents each bought us one pack of 1987 Topps. I had never seen a pack of cards before, but hey, why not try opening one? As I unwrapped the bright green wax wrapper, I was surprised to find a stick of gum included. Actually, calling it gum would be a stretch. Perhaps it would be best to call it a gum-flavored piece of plastic, that when bitten into, would shatter into 50 sugary razor-sharp pieces designed to rip your tongue to shreds. A 1987 Topps Danny Tartabull would have probably been healthier to consume!

As we opened our packs, Charlie was excited about a card he pulled of the National League Rookie of the Year winner Todd Worrell. This card was different from the others, as it had a cool little cartoon gold cup in the corner. I opened my pack up and got a different card with the same cup. My card depicted a man in a bright green Athletics jersey who happened to be the American League Rookie of the Year, Jose Canseco.

Charlie was insistent that we trade rookie cup cards. He was very eager to do the deal. A little too eager. His intense excitement got this young boy's brain to thinking that perhaps it wouldn't be such a good deal for me, no matter how much he may have wanted me to think Worrell was better than Canseco.

With as many attempts as he made, I stayed strong to the end and decided not to make the trade. I felt like I had won, though I wasn't sure why. I still didn't fully understand why people would collect these small pictures of men playing a game anyway, even though the wood borders did look cool.

As with everything that wasn't related to dinosaurs or Nintendo at the time, I threw the cards into the junk drawer in my room and forgot about them.

When I got into baseball cards a couple of years later in 1989, I searched for the 1987 Topps I remembered I had carelessly tossed into the drawer. After a few minutes of searching, I found them. More importantly, I found the Jose Canseco card. I remembered hearing others talking about him, as he was the best baseball player on the planet. It all started to sink in. I had the rookie cup card of the guy who hit 42 home runs and stole 40 bases in the same season. Surely, I hit the jackpot!

As my love for baseball grew, my favorite team seemed like they were unbeatable, which fueled my interest even more. In 1989, the Oakland Athletics were on a tear and railroaded nearly everyone that got in their way. Unfortunately, Canseco was sidelined for the better part of the season. I still remember sitting at Wendy's during lunch when my parents told me about his injury - how it would keep him out of baseball for quite a while. That was a very hard thing to hear as a new fan.

Thankfully, he came back at the end of the season and clobbered 17 home runs in 65 games. Exactly the kind of thing you would expect a baseball jersey wearing superhero to do. With Canseco's bat back in the lineup and Rickey Henderson coming back to Oakland where he belonged, the Oakland Athletics routed the San Francisco Giants in the World Series by sweeping them.

FRIENDS AND RIVALS

Being a fan and baseball card collector in the late '80s was as easy as it was popular. Just down the street, Nick and Bryan were die-hard Giants fans. They were brothers who were within a few years of my age and both loved Will "The Thrill" Clark and Kevin Mitchell. Bryan had a super thick binder full of Giants cards, which he would spend hours organizing and maintaining.

We would have countless sleepovers and constantly trade cards. If I opened any packs of cards and got Giants, I would trade them for their A's cards they pulled. Not all deals were easy, though. I specifically remember one time when they came over, and showed me something truly beautiful. A Mother's Cookies card of Jose Canseco ... one that I didn't have!

I didn't know how much it was worth, and I didn't know what it was going to take, but I knew I had to have it. The Mother's Cookies cards were special. They featured a high gloss, full-color photograph with no artwork and rounded corners. The crisp, friendly photography and bright colors would always remind me of the best time of year: Spring Training. The back of each card boasted a spot for the player to sign. This always puzzled me, though. Who in their right mind would have their favorite player sign the back of the card, anyway?

I put together a number of trade options, and they denied each offer smugly, as to say "we have something you want badly, but can't get!"

Then, my dad came into the room.

"Hey, Tanner - I picked up some Mother's Cookies and I know he isn't your guy, but here is the card that came in the package."

The card was a Will Clark. One that neither Nick or Bryan had!

My, how sweet it was to have control. After proudly showing my new card to them, I knew that the tables had turned. Would they be willing to deal the Canseco I needed AND another card? As it turned out, they were, so I landed some great prizes that day. Thanks, dad!

Speaking of Mother's Cookies, our pantry was filled with packages of them, much to my mom's chagrin. Dad and I would go out all the time to get them. A dealer friend told us that #2 of 4 in the Nolan Ryan set was "the rare one" and told us which package on the Costco's pallet would have it. That is about as close to pack searching as we got. Other people, however, were quite a bit more creative. Back then, we heard stories of how people would bring metal detectors to Costco to detect if any of the 1991 Donruss cases had an Elite Series card. It has been said that others were able to find loads of 1992 Donruss Elite cards simply by plucking out the lighter colored packs from display boxes.

MAKING THE GRADE

My parents found out that baseball cards were a huge motivator for my grades. In the midst of report cards full of C's, mom and dad told me for every A I received, they would give me $10, and $5 for every B. For the first time in my life, I had all the motivation I needed to be at the top of my class. When the very next 5th-grade report card came out for yours truly, guess what? I got straight A's. That meant $80 for me to spend on baseball cards.

With that kind of money burning a hole in my pocket, I was extremely excited for the weekend to come when my parents would routinely take me to my favorite place in the world: The Bullpen. After drooling over the cards in the display cases, I pulled out my carefully thought out list and cast my gaze upon the countless wax pack offerings displayed on the shelves anchored to the walls that were calling my name.

My order was much like a chef calling for ingredients. My game plan was to mix quality with quantity, and I did just that. "Yes, I'll take two packs of 1982 Fleer, eight packs of 1988 Donruss, twelve packs of 1987 Topps, five packs of 1989 Upper Deck ..."

"Wow, this is like Christmas for you!" The dealer Mike told me.

Mike's words could not have been truer. When I got home, I pulled out the upper left drawer in my desk and placed the packs there to enjoy the anticipation of what riches awaited me inside of the colorful wax wrappers. There's just something about having a messy array of wax packs from various years, colors and brands that I enjoyed having at my disposal. They probably remained sealed for about a week.

Confessions of a Baseball Card Addict

When it was time to open the packs, I carefully pulled them out of my desk drawer, and brought them to the living room, placing them in stacks on the coffee table. I sat down at the couch and cracked my knuckles. *It's go time.*

While I recall being disappointed because I didn't find anything great in the packs, I find it interesting that I remember all of the events leading up to opening the packs so vividly. The report card, the trip to the card shop. Heck, I even remember the dealer Mike putting the packs in a long, slender, transparent bag. It goes to show you that this hobby has always reached far beyond the confines of simply acquiring cards for your collection. It is also about the journey.

The report card after that was more of the same, grades wise. School wasn't so bad after all! Unfortunately, my parents pulled the plug shortly after that, because they had some wild notion that keeping the lights on at home and food on the table was more important than baseball cards. I immediately went back to a steady diet of getting C's.

THE SON OF A JANITOR

Growing up, my parents ran a janitorial business. While the rest of the world was humming along at their jobs from 9 to 5, my parents were preparing to clean their offices during the night. This meant that occasionally, my nights would be spent sleeping on the floor of office complexes and being moved from a car dealership to a meat packing building, to a bank, until the work was done. Floors would be waxed, desks dusted and wastebaskets emptied. Being in a foreign office complex, bank or car dealership after hours was an eerie feeling. With all of the empty offices and desks, it almost felt like I was the last person on earth.

It was fun being up later than other kids my age and was an experience I'll never forget. I was also put to work sometimes - even by cleaning the women's bathroom. A strange feeling for a 10 to 12-year-old boy, even though the entire complex would have been completely vacant of all people for hours at that point. My parents assured me it was okay since no one else was around. Putting me to work meant extra money to buy baseball cards, so I figured I would bend my standards just a bit.

On occasion, mom & dad would buy me an entire box of baseball cards and a baseball card magazine, to keep me occupied while they were working at night. This alone made any situation seem like the best thing ever. Oftentimes, I would be in a sleeping bag on the hard industrial carpet of some boardroom, happily opening packs of 1990 Topps.

When I was done, I would sort them, and then read from Beckett Monthly. Without any super-hot cards or inserts to chase, I don't think I was really hoping to pull anything valuable. It was just such a fun time to open an entire box and enjoy each card to the fullest. I still remember the smell of the gum, and the excitement of pulling one card away to reveal the card behind it. Enjoying the bright, colorful borders, and looking at the stats on the back of the cards to see who had a better year. It was perfect.

On the nights we didn't have to go anywhere, I would go to sleep dreaming of baseball cards. What would it be like opening an entire case of 1989 Score baseball cards? How cool would it be to have a Jose Canseco autograph? Better yet - what if Canseco came to my birthday party? Now that would be something!

I ended up sending an autograph request and invited him to my birthday party. It took a lot of courage to do, but I mailed my prized 1989 Fleer baseball card of him to autograph, with the worry that it may be lost forever. To give my card the best chance of survival, I decided to wrap it in cellophane. Several months later, to my surprise, it came back to me in the mail! I opened it up, and Jose had signed it. Unfortunately, he signed it right on top of the cellophane. To add insult to injury, he was a no-show for my birthday party.

CANSECO GETS TRADED

On the morning of September 1st, 1992, my mom woke me up with some terrible news.

"So, do you think hose-head will like it in Texas?"

Still dazed from just waking up, I asked what she meant.

"Last night, Canseco was traded to the Rangers."

"Shut up!" I told my mom ... and then started crying. That was the first and only time I ever snapped at her like that, but can you blame me? Canseco was traded from the A's to the Rangers, and she clearly wasn't taking this tragedy seriously enough! This took her by surprise, and she immediately understood the gravity of the situation for me, so she graciously let it slide.

I made the false assumption that I would be given the day off to stay at home from school to mourn this earth-shattering news, but mom did not agree. I put on my best Jose Canseco shirt commemorating his 40/40 season as a tribute to the man who was so ruthlessly ripped from the best team on the planet all too soon.

This was all so confusing for me. What team do I root for now? The A's or Rangers? What happens when they play against each other? With all this uncertainty, one thing remained the same: No matter what team he played for, Canseco would always be my favorite player. This is something that probably discouraged my parents to no end because the man would regularly make newspaper headlines thanks to his unscrupulous (or perhaps misunderstood) extra-curricular activities.

It took a while, but I finally made peace with the fact that Jose had departed to Texas. It still felt like a divorce to me, but I distinctly remember cutting up some logo stickers that came in

Fleer wax packs of the A's and Rangers. I cut them into four pieces and alternated them to make one Frankenstein logo to display on the inside back flap of the binder that housed my Canseco collection. Today, this binder is used by my son Atticus for his collection with the Frankensticker still in-tact.

MOVING TO TEXAS

It wasn't long until my family decided to go the way of Canseco and move to Texas ourselves when I was in junior high. We started out life in Houston in a bad section of town.

We found out that the annual baseball card show in Texas was going to have Jose Canseco there for a signing. Words cannot describe how huge of news this was for me. I begged and pleaded with my parents to go. To my delight, they agreed!

When we got there, it was surreal knowing that my hero, the player who was the face of baseball, was in the same building I was in.

As they called us up, there he was: sitting at a table in his street clothes. The only thing between my hero and me was about ten zigzag rows marked off by velvet ropes used to organize and direct a soon to be overflowing crowd. As one of the first people there, I quickly shuffled left down the first row, right down the second row, left again down the third row, and continued until I got to the table. All I could do was stare and give him my 8x10 picture of him on the Rangers to sign. He quickly signed in black right across his leg.

"Wow, thank you, Mr. Canseco!"

He responded with a little smirk and a nod. *"S'alright."*

Mom tells me it was a nightmare to get back home. It took us over two hours because we got lost and then got stuck in horrible traffic, but I don't remember any of that. I was too star struck.

"He said something to me, mom!"

Confessions of a Baseball Card Addict

They Call it Cardboard Crack

Did You Know?

The 1985 Topps baseball card of former Angels Outfielder Gary Pettis actually depicts his 16 year old brother, Lynn Pettis.

Ah, the excitement a baseball card dealer must feel each day! I thought it must be pure, unadulterated bliss. I had dreams of sleeping in the back of my own baseball card shop and waking up to the smell of 1989 Upper Deck in the morning. I would then plant my feet on the sacred ground that is behind the glass display cases. The next order of business would be to select a few choice wax packs that I could open up over breakfast while enjoying the current Beckett magazine, much like adults would read the newspaper in the morning.

The rest of the day would only get better. Friends would come in and out of my shop to buy and trade cards, or just chat. A baseball game would be on in the background for our enjoyment, and everyone would be drooling over all of the wax packs and singles I had for sale. There would be many conversations about baseball cards and speculation on which way the arrows would be pointing for certain cards in the next price guide. That's what my ten-year-old brain came up with as the perfect life, anyway.

As a child, my obsession with baseball cards added color to otherwise black and white memories. I vividly remember riding in the car with my parents when I was sick, and they stopped by a shop to pick up three packs of 1989 Fleer for 75 cents each. I remember seeing the house we were going to move into for the first time one Saturday morning, but only because of the baseball cards that were in my lap. I can't tell you anything else about the day other than the full wax box of 1989 Topps and loose packs of "Eight Men Out" I had. I remember opening them at the kitchen table in front of my uncle Jeff and loving the 1989 Topps Future Star cards. I also remember not caring much for the Eight Men Out cards with the maroon borders framing pictures of actors. Why would I care about them? Neither Gary Sheffield nor Greg Jefferies could be found in those packs.

I also remember the time when I decided to plunk down $18 for a box of 1990 Fleer at a local shop - the A's game was on

TV in the shop, and the Brewers were blowing them out by scoring in the double digits. The anticipation of opening the box of Fleer somehow made that atrocity better. Who knew what treasures would be in the box? David Justice or Kevin Maas perhaps?

1991 Donruss brings back memories of a Christmas Tree farm near my childhood home, and how I sat in the back seat with five unopened packs, marveling at the border color change between series one and two.

THE BULLPEN

I think that my desire to become a baseball card dealer can largely be blamed on my favorite place in the world: The Bullpen. It was the best baseball card shop around, and I always looked forward to going there each Saturday. It was about a 10-minute drive from home, so it was just out of reach by bike, but close enough that my parents would indulge my addiction on a weekly basis. Saturday was the best day of the week for me, for this very reason. Next to Canseco, the owner Mike was my hero.

The Bullpen was located in a one-story shopping strip complex. The room was longer than it was wide, and was lined with glass cases situated in a U shape. These glass cases artfully displayed the best cards that you could purchase. I am sure that they sold basketball, football, and hockey cards, but they didn't matter to me one bit. For me, it was all about the baseball cards.

Just like many other card shops, the Bullpen had shelves on the wall that displayed a plethora of wax boxes. Each had prices that were handwritten on bright poster board showing the cost of each pack, and the key cards you could pull from them. While 50 cents was the going rate for most new packs at the time, there were some packs for the high rollers: 1990 Leaf for $5, 1987 Fleer for $7, and 1986 Donruss for $10.

Buying packs for such high prices were what one could consider gambling. Now and then, you would have someone come into the shop to throw down some money on the glass case and open a pack for everyone to see. If they hit something big, they were the man. If not, they walked away, hanging their head in shame, often leaving the worthless pile of commons on the case.

The only time I remember my dad doing this was at another shop named Baseball Greats, owned and operated by Ronnie, a church friend. Dad decided to throw down $7 on a pack of 1987 Fleer and opened it in front of everyone. I remember having the distinct feeling that mom should probably not know about this. He flipped the blue wax pack over, and skillfully undid the wax flaps to reveal the cards. All eyes were on him - could he pull a Barry Bonds? Bo Jackson? Will Clark? Kevin Mitchell? Bobby Bonilla? Jose Canseco? Each pack gave you 17 tries at one of these "jackpot" cards. Card by card, hope dwindled until it was a certainty that the best card in the pack was the free sticker that was included.

While it is true that most people gambling this way hardly ever won, Mike, the owner at the Bullpen decided to try his luck one Saturday while we were at his shop. Cool as a cucumber, he pulled a single pack from the untouchable (to me) 1990 Leaf Series 2 box that was on the shelf that anyone could have picked from and purchased. He unwrapped the pack, quickly shuffled through the cards and pulled out a 1990 Leaf Frank Thomas rookie card, just like a magician who would have pulled a rabbit out of his hat. After showing it to everyone, he put it in the glass display case with a five dollar price tag. He recommended that someone buy it now, as he predicted it would increase in value for the next 12 months consecutively. To my best recollection, it did! The Thomas ended up being one of the hottest cards of its time.

After a while, I decided to pause buying new cards and asked Mike if he had any older cards from the '60s and '70s. No kids asked about these cards ever, but they were intriguing to me. There was just something about collecting cards of players that were before my time that interested me. For several months in a row, during my routine Saturday Bullpen run, I would make the rounds by ritualistically ogling over the cards in the cases and wax boxes on the wall for about thirty minutes. When I was done, I would ask Mike to bring out the box of vintage cards to look through. Mike would disappear to the back office - a magical place with untold treasures.

After returning from the back office, he would carefully place a five-row wooden box of vintage cards on the glass case for me to thumb through. I would generally pick a few commons or semi-stars to spend my allowance on and happily make my way back out to the car where my mom and/or dad were waiting for me.

INTRODUCING PRODIGY

Back in the early '90s, I would make trades with my friends, but that was only a network of about five or ten kids. My parents signed up for an "online membership" called Prodigy. This was back in 1990 and was well before the mainstream internet made its way into houses all over the world. Actually, I wasn't aware of too many houses that even had computers back then. For all I knew, everyone might have, but they just weren't important to kids and had absolutely nothing to do with our day to day lives as they do now.

Prodigy was a new way of connecting with people all over the world and was life-changing for me. It helped me to connect with others right from the comfort of home, but more importantly, it opened me up to a whole other world of collecting and dealing. As a ten-year-old eager to make some deals, I remember sitting in the kitchen and firing up the old monochrome monitor, waiting to be welcomed by a command prompt. I would tap away and open up Prodigy. When connecting, you would hear the familiar buzzing, popping and zinging sounds of the modem. The username and password would be input, and in a couple of minutes, I was connected with people from all over the world. A world filled with people of all ages, shapes, sizes, and races conversing back and forth with each other. It didn't matter how old anyone was, what they looked like or how they sounded. It was a vibrant, buzzing world that was completely anonymous, without the use of graphics.

I was mesmerized by the orange glow of the text that appeared on the screen. It would list topic after topic of people I didn't know who had cards for trade. To me, this was as addictive as Nintendo was, if not more. It wasn't just about cards, though. It was about dealing with other people. Since Prodigy did not allow any form of sales, we would speak in code. If someone had a 1987 Topps Will Clark that they wanted to sell for $3, they would say it was for trade for 3 GWRCs. That was code for $3 (Three George Washington Rookie Cards).

Eventually, I started making several deals a day and had so many things going at one time, I had to keep notes. An olive green hinged metal box would serve as my Rolodex, and in it were index cards of various colors, each with valuable information. One side of each index card would have the name and address of the customer I was dealing with, and the other side would have complete details of the transaction. This would include the date of the deal, what the deal was, and the date the money and/or cards were received. At the beginning of each day, there would be a line of packages ready to go out in the mail on our ledge, and at the end of each day, a pile of packages addressed to me would come in. Each mail day felt like Christmas.

Generally, these deals would go off without a hitch, but every now and then, there would be a swindler that would take advantage of the serious flaws in pre-internet mail trading. Perhaps the one that hurt the most for me back then was when I struck a deal with someone for my complete set of 1982 Donruss. I loved that set, but I loved the 1953 Topps Satchel Paige and Warren Spahn that was offered to me even more.

I sent out the 1982 Donruss set without any worries or concerns something would go wrong. The 1953 Topps cards finally came in, and something immediately felt off with them. They had a glossy finish and were the same size as today's standard sized cards, not the size of the 1953 Topps cards. I was duped with a couple of reprints from the 1991 Topps Archives series.

As time went on, I was told of an impending doom. Prodigy would start limiting everyone to 30 free emails a month, and after that, you would have to pay 25 cents per email. I knew that this would mean the end of the line for my little business, as I would routinely burn through 30 emails within a few days.

SMALL TOWN BUSINESS

When we moved to Kansas, not only did we not have Prodigy, we had no computer at all. I had to figure out a way to stay in the hobby that I loved so much and was making me more money than my little car wash business did in California. At 12 years old, it was during this time that my passion for baseball card collecting spread like wildfire across Robinson.

In the short time I lived there, I made converts of almost every school-aged boy in town. In doing so, I racked up about $400 cash from selling to them during the summer, which was a fortune to me. It was also a much more desirable way to make money than the way the older boy across the street took by mowing lawns. He was known as the junior entrepreneur of the town and had built up quite the client base. I hold fast to the fact that I'd rather make $20 selling baseball cards than mowing someone's lawn. 1992 Fleer Ultra has always smelled better to me than freshly cut grass.

While I didn't have any online access, I did have magazines that I could use to purchase cards through mail order. During my time in Kansas, I saved up my money to purchase a 1958 Topps All-Star Mickey Mantle, 1960 Topps Stan Musial, and 1961 Topps MVP Mickey Mantle. The '61 Mantle was severely off-center, but I loved it anyway. I found these cards for sale in a price list from a magazine, mailed a check off and in several weeks, I got my first big money vintage cards ever. They probably cost me $250 in total. I had to push a LOT of 1992 Topps to make that kind of scratch! It is laughable to think that this is how card purchases through the mail happened back then. Nowadays, you can purchase a card from California on Monday, have it arrive Wednesday morning and sell it to someone in Japan by lunch!

One day, my parents decided we were going to go to a bookstore in the mall. As I was there, I found a book called *Mr. Mint's Insider's Guide to Investing in Baseball Cards and Collectibles*. I loved that book so much, and read it more than any other book I had ever read before. This fired me up even further to get into dealing baseball cards and buying vintage.

One thing my parents had me listen to previously was Zig Ziglar's "Goals: Setting them and Achieving Them on Schedule." At 12 years old, I used the techniques learned from this taped lecture to save up enough money to purchase 25 T-206 tobacco cards from a Kit Young catalog. It was an absolute dream to have them, but several years later, I ended up selling them very cheaply on eBay to have money for a Christmas present for my fiancé who is now my wife. Even though I miss those T-206 cards, I'd say it was a worthwhile investment!

YOUR FRIENDLY, NEIGHBORHOOD CARDBOARD CRACK DEALER

In almost every television show that has to do with school, there is a character who sells drugs to kids in private. In 7th grade, I was that dealer. The drug? Baseball cards, or what a dealer friend of mine named Dwain called them: Cardboard crack. Before school, I would run to the gas station and buy up as many packs of cards as I could afford, then stuff them in my trapper keeper and backpack.

I would haul my precious cargo from class to class, and would be flagged down by kids itching for a Stadium Club high. During the lunch hour, I would have a line of kids at my table with their lunch money in hand to buy the packs I had for sale. I was responsible for all of the disruptive stomach growls throughout the rest of the afternoon, because the boys liked wax packs more than they liked lunch.

I always sold out, and had plenty of money to re-invest into wax packs to sell for the next day, plus a few extra packs for me to enjoy - for free! As fate would have it, one of my junior high customers named Jonathan recognized me at a baseball card show about 20 years later, and ended up becoming my son's youth pastor!

JUNK WAX FOR VINTAGE

The next year, I met an older guy who was of driving age. Nick was very tall, would wear a large jacket and had his ear pierced. Aside from that, he seemed very clean cut, so the ensemble threw me off. It seemed as though Nick was from a different planet, but cardboard has a tendency of uniting people from all walks of life. He told me he had a friend with a bunch of older cards from the '50s and '60s and would be willing to trade for several of the complete sets I had amassed over the years.

When Nick told me to come over, we both loaded up many of my complete sets and went to his townhouse. Waiting for us was his friend Greg, who I would classify as a man. He made mention that he was engaged to be married, and had "man stubble". A five o'clock shadow was prevalent. It felt a bit strange, almost like a setup. I had people try to rip me off before, so I was on high alert. They outnumbered me and were considerably older, but thanks to practically memorizing the Beckett price guide each month, I was well versed in card values, so I was not worried. My past experiences with reprints also kept me alert.

We laid my complete sets out on the bed in Nick's room. 1988 Donruss, 1988 Fleer, 1989 Topps, 1990 Fleer, 1990 Score, 1991 Donruss, and others. They would all be considered nowadays as junk wax sets. With my complete sets laid out, Greg couldn't hide the huge smile on his face. With his gaze fixed on my cards, he handed me his box of old cards. All of them were in card savers, and all were from the '50s and '60s just like Nick told me! As I looked at them, I had a smile I couldn't hide either. I shuffled through them and made mental notes of all I was seeing.

There were several different cards from various sets such as 1951 Topps blue & red backs, 1962 Topps, 1955 Bowman, 1963 Fleer, 1953 Topps, 1954 Bowman, 1954 Topps, and even 1952 Topps! The very thought that I was holding several cards from the set that the famed 1952 Topps Mickey Mantle card came from was exhilarating - like I was holding pieces of baseball card history. They were in rough shape, but definitely real and were much more desirable to me than the complete sets that had been staring back at me from my closet for years.

I ended up trading Greg all of the complete sets I brought over for his entire box of vintage baseball cards. The overt snickering and looks Greg and Nick were giving each other the whole time was a huge tell that they thought they were pulling

Confessions of a Baseball Card Addict

one over on the poor, seemingly clueless kid. I don't recall ever seeing or hearing from either of them again, but that was the best trade I had made up to that point in my life. They gave me years of enjoyment, and I loved showing my friends cards that were several decades older than they were. They made a great conversation piece! As an adult, I sold them for significantly more than I would have ever gotten for the sets.

CARD SHOW FLIPPING

Going to baseball card shows was magical. You didn't have just one dealer; you had fifty or more. It was like an endless treasure hunt. This is where I could really sink my teeth into getting several Canseco cards that I didn't yet have. I recall reading an article in Beckett magazine on how to best scout out a show. The article gave tactical and strategic advice on how to navigate through the tables and target good deals.

One of my earliest experiences was finding a table that was run by an older man and woman. They had several rows of cards in boxes that were separated by player. I quickly shuffled to the Canseco cards, and after about 20 minutes, I emerged from the cardboard with a nice large pile of Canseco cards I didn't have. I was incredibly excited, and surely they would work on price with me, right? Wrong.

"Excuse me, ma'am?" I said. "I am interested in these Canseco cards. Would you consider $9 for them?"

She peered at me over her glasses and into my soul as I handed her the pile. She quickly shuffled through them as if I had insulted her by merely being in her presence. The woman then sharply snorted and called to her husband.

"Did you hear that Rob? This kid wants to get all of these for $9."

It must have really tickled them because they laughed like a couple of villains plotting a heist. By doing this, they sent me the message loud and clear that the deal wasn't happening. I walked away with my tail between my legs, and onto the next dealer. They must have really wanted that extra $4.

Things weren't always like this, though. I learned how to adapt and how to handle the various personalities I would encounter from table to table. One of my favorite things to do at a card show would be to purchase cards from one dealer and sell them for a profit to another dealer a few tables down. The first time I did this was with a few vintage cards. I was with my dad, and he stood by as a silent observer. I showed him what I had bought - a few 1952 Topps baseball cards, and a few minutes later, I sold them to another dealer for a quick $25 profit. Doing this at an early age helped me to learn how to deal with people, as I'd have to face rejection and ridicule ten times before getting to that sweet, sweet "yes".

One of my last memories of dealing cards as a kid had to have been as a 13-year-old. I posted up an ad in the newspaper stating I had wax boxes for sale. A much older man responded and said he was interested. I asked my parents if it would be okay to meet with this man at Jack in the Box, and they agreed - as long as they could sit a few tables down to supervise. I felt like a big shot doing a historic deal like they do in the movies. I dressed the part by putting on my best turtleneck (this was the '90s, remember?) and met the man with my wax boxes in my arms. I was able to sell a lot of cards to him that day, and I walked out of restaurant feeling like a big-time dealer. Then reality hit me that I was still just a kid, as I was told to hop in the back seat of my parent's car so we could go home and I could finish up my homework.

END OF AN ERA

Like most kids that grew up collecting in the late '80s / early '90s, I slowly drifted away from the hobby that I loved so much. I started devoting my time to friends, girls, cars and church youth group activities. As time went on, the memories I had locked up in my cards made it harder and harder for me to continue selling, so I gave up on dealing and kept my treasures stored away in my closet, rarely even to be thought of over the next several years.

Wow. Man-Crush Much?

Did You Know?

The name Donruss is a combination of the founder's names Don and Russ Weiner.

To say that a lot happened over the next decade of my life would be an understatement. Baseball cards just weren't on my radar. To that point, if you aren't interested in my life away from the hobby, I invite you to flip to page 33. If you do have an interest in what I was up to during my cardboard hiatus, feel free to press on.

As I entered high school at the age of 14, I got in with the wrong crowd and acted in such a way that was contrary to my Christian upbringing. I tried hard to "be good", but just couldn't. I was ashamed and felt convicted. One night, I broke down and asked God to forgive me and thanked Him for sending His Son Jesus to die for my sins. It felt like a huge weight had been lifted off of my shoulders.

Shortly after this, I got heavily involved at church and the youth group where I made some lifelong friends. There were about 15 or 20 of us that did everything together. For years, these friends were a big part of my life, and we loved hanging out with each other throughout high school. As I write this, my son Atticus is now in high school and is also enjoying the same type of close friendships in his youth group just as I did over twenty years ago at the very same church!

ENTERING THE WORKFORCE

Ever since I was 16, I have been working. At one point, I worked three jobs at the same time. The church hired me on as a maintenance and event setup guy, while I also worked at a bookstore and Chic-Fil-A in the mall. Fridays were long for me, as I would hitch a ride with dad (he worked at Foley's in the mall) to get to work at Chic-Fil-A at 7:30 in the morning. I would get off at 12 and have lunch in the food court. From there, I would change in the bathroom and walk down the left wing of the mall to work at the bookstore until 9:30.

Later on, I signed up at a temp agency. The main skill I brought to the table was that I could type fast. Really fast. Over the next couple of years, I was placed on assignment in over a dozen different companies. The jobs were quite varied, to say the least. One company used me as a mystery shopper to place orders at several restaurants around town and report back to headquarters to tell them how well each one performed. That was fun until one of the restaurant managers tried to chase me down in his car.

WHEN GOD TOLD ME TO MOVE BACK TO TEXAS

With my parents telling me they were going to move back to California at the end of 1999, I knew that everything was going to change drastically, and I had to plan for my future. As a 19 year old, the plan was to follow my mom out west and move to Arizona with my friend Blake, while she continued driving to California in her car to reunite with dad who had moved back a few months prior. As the Bible says in Proverbs 19:21: *"Many are the plans in a person's heart, but it is the Lord's purpose that prevails."* And along came Holly.

Holly, a beautiful 18-year-old, first caught my eye one Thursday evening. We met at a deaf ministry, and as a sign language student in college, she attended this event for extra credit. I showed up because a friend of mine invited me. She never came, but thankfully, Holly and I hit it off. Though we grew close over the next few months, the time came for me to move. I packed up everything I owned in my pride and joy - my Camaro - and mom packed up everything she owned in her car.

Through about a week's worth of tears from both of us, I said goodbye forever to the most beautiful girl I had ever seen. Since I thought this was what I was supposed to do with my life, I made the long trek westward, and followed mom out of town. As He does with many things in my life, God had other plans. About six hours into the journey, mom abruptly pulled over in the middle of nowhere and called me.

"What is wrong?" I asked mom.

"My car died. The engine started making a horrible knocking sound, and it just quit," she responded.

So there we were, off the side of the road in the middle of nowhere, with everything we owned and a morbidly obese cat of 25 pounds. How could this be? She took it to the mechanic to get it fully checked out just a few days before to make sure nothing like this would happen.

I prayed to God and asked that if He wanted me to move back to Texas, to please have my mom ask me about moving back. I have no idea why I prayed that, as it wasn't even a thought in my mind. No more than 10 seconds later, mom got out of the car and walked over to me.

"Well, I don't know kiddo. What do you think about moving back to Texas?"

My jaw dropped out of amazement. Why would she ask such a thing? I told her that God just told me to, so I did. Because both of our cars were filled to the brim, I had to move all of the baseball cards that were in my passenger seat to her driver seat to make room for her and her cat.

We left her car filled all of her belongings and my baseball card collection on the side of the road then drove back to Houston. Grandpa flew out and rented a U-Haul to pick my mom up and trailer her broken down car back to California. Thankfully, no one stole her car or my collection. The very next day, I walked back into Holly's life at her sister's birthday party, and we got married a year and a half later. We have been inseparable ever since and have been married for 17 years!

BEING HOMELESS

Though coming back to Houston is what I felt God wanted me to do, I didn't have a place to stay, a job to work at or any sort of safety net, whatsoever. In just a short period of time,

I went from living at home with my parents to being homeless. It felt like I had to grow up overnight.

Thankfully, it wasn't too long before I was able to find a job and a place to live. My new home was a tiny one bedroom apartment behind a dumpster. This is where I started my own business while working at a job that I hated.

With as much motivation as I could muster, I poured my heart and soul into learning how to build websites. I made up fliers and went door to door handing them out at businesses all over the place during my lunch break. I was desperate to find a way to leave the job that made me so miserable. I had a few takers for my door to door venture, but nothing I could support myself on. Long gone, were the innocent days of dreaming Canseco would come to my birthday party, and becoming a baseball card dealer.

As a 19-year-old young man, I can safely say that the living and working situation I found myself in was a nightmarish way to start adulthood. My one bedroom apartment was scary, to say the least. Over the years, they found a few dead bodies in the complex. Finances were incredibly tight, and living on ramen noodle soup was the norm. This was all livable though, and I didn't have much of a problem with this at the time, so long as one of the dead bodies wasn't me! One day, my neighbor suggested I sleep on the floor that night due to rumors of a drive-by shooting.

I was miserable working under an extremely difficult boss, and the bright spot of every day was when Holly would come over after I got home from work. It was on a bright and sunny afternoon in May of 2000 that I left the job of misery, forever. As I left, I had concerns about being able to make rent. That feeling was vastly overshadowed by the liberating feeling of getting out of the job I hated. With no job and very little money,

I did what any young man would do. I asked Holly to be my wife.

That night, I took her to the fountain where we had our first date, got my guitar out and played the song I wrote her. The last line of the song was *"Will you marry me?"* I presented her with a meager engagement ring that I bought using a credit card. Thankfully, she said yes!

LEARNING HOW TO ADULT

Not only was I unemployed and nearly broke; I also now had a fiancé. Things definitely had to change, but I wasn't sure how. I spent all of my time trying to land web design projects on my own and came up with a few. With only a few weeks' worth of money in the bank to live on, I was in dire straits. One night at a youth group function I was helping out at, we had a missionary speaker named Doug.

Doug was like a rock star. Everyone knew him, and his story. He was in the Air Force and later the FBI. He had an incredible testimony and was a very engaging speaker. After the event, he came up and spoke with me, asking how life was going. I told him my situation, and he pointed me to a 29-year-old man named Chris who had left his job to start a web design company.

Doug set up a lunch meeting with Chris and me, which went very well. Chris had me come over to his house for a one on one meeting a few nights later. We spoke at length about many things, and he decided to give me a chance. After our first meeting, I walked out of his house with a $3,000 check to get started on two projects that needed to be done in about two months. Imagine how many packs of baseball cards I could have bought if it weren't for those pesky bills!

This was significantly more money than I had ever made before at one time, and though I knew it was meant to cover two months living expenses, I felt like all my problems were erased by this man's belief in me - and his check. Not only was I free from driving 45 minutes each way to go to a job I hated, but I was also able to work doing something I liked, and from home!

For the next several months, I worked very hard to keep my status as a self-employed web designer working from home. Chris became my business mentor and big brother, as his business acumen and work ethic rubbed off on me. He had me work on websites for his clients while I was landing my own projects as well, until he went back to work at his previous company about a year and a half later. It was very worrisome to me that I would have to make a go of it all alone - especially since I was to be getting married in a couple of months!

With Chris gone, I could only rely on what projects I could land personally. Within a couple of weeks, I met with an organization about a website and walked away with a $9,500 contract - wildly more than I had ever made from any other single project! Thanks to this contract, I was able to move out of the scary apartment behind the dumpster, and into a much nicer apartment complex to start married life without the worry of being gunned down in a drive-by.

Remembering my former miserable living and work situation was all the motivation I needed to work as hard as I could to continue to be my own boss. I was reminded of how thankful I should be a couple of years later when I was driving on my way to meet with a client. This project would yield more money than the job I hated would have paid me in an entire year. While I was thinking about this, I looked out my window and had to laugh. As fate would have it, I was driving right by my former place of employment to get to my meeting! That building never looked so good as it did getting smaller and smaller from my rear-view mirror that day.

OUR NEW FAMILY

Shortly after Holly and I got married, the greatest thing ever happened to us - we got pregnant! On October 22nd, 2002, our son Atticus came into the world. He is the best thing that has ever happened to us - God has spoiled us rotten with him. At the time of this writing, he is 16 years old, is taller than me and has a deeper voice than I do. We are extremely proud of the young man he is becoming.

A few years after Atticus was born, we became homeowners. While our house was nothing like a mansion, I was very proud of it because it was ours. A few months after moving in, Hurricane Rita hit Houston. Thankfully, when all was said and done, our house had no damage, though a lot of our area of town looked like a war zone.

REMINISCING ABOUT BASEBALL CARDS AGAIN

Without power due to the hurricane, I thought I would pass the time by pulling out my Jose Canseco collection for the first time in years. I made my way up the stairs and started rummaging around in the dark of my closet to look for them. I found them in a nice small box and binder - the binder I had placed the Frankensticker with the A's/Rangers logo on.

I brought them downstairs into the living room and started laying them all out on the table to sort them. It brought back many fond memories! For years, I was focused on my family and the business, which didn't leave much time to reminisce about my childhood. It was great to see the 1987 Topps Rookie Cup card again, as well as the 1990 Topps card that helped me get an A on my report about Florida as a child.

As I was sitting there having the time of my life, my sister-in-law Brittany came over, looked at what had to be 300 Canseco cards, then looked at me and said

"Wow. Man-crush much?"

An unusual feeling of embarrassment came over me, but then I realized that I was basically caught red-handed, and was truly enjoying myself. Though it probably looked differently to her, my enjoyment didn't come from Canseco himself, but rather the cards.

For the first time in over ten years, I found my love for baseball cards again. This time, however, I had money to spend...and eBay. Armed with these two things I didn't have as a child, I set out for a collecting goal. I thought it would be great to collect one of every major baseball card set from the year I was born in 1980 all the way up until I had stopped heavily collecting as a child. What a great and fun goal that would be! Surely, it would be a fairly cheap endeavor. How fun to have rookies of all the players I watched growing up, and then some.

DEFINING THE CARDBOARD RELATIONSHIP

If you have ever set a collecting goal, you know what comes next: DTCR (Defining the Cardboard Relationship). What did I want to go after, and what did I want to pass up? Should I collect only the full sets? What about the traded/update sets? Should I only go for them in factory form? What about the little-boxed sets from K-Mart? 7-Eleven coins? What about regionally issued team sets? How about minor league cards? This quickly went from sounding like a fun little hobby that would fit in my closet, to a daunting and expensive endeavor that could fill up our entire house.

I started picking up some complete sets haphazardly, enjoying the significant disparity between how much they were priced at and how much they used to cost, but cringing over the cost of shipping. It all seemed to balance out though. I don't know if this endeavor was a way to relive my childhood, or to make 12 year old me jealous. But either way, it brought back all sorts of memories. I kept thinking how amazing it would have been to have had the 1980 Topps set as a kid, and now I could easily obtain one. Or how I could get back the 1982 Donruss set I was ripped off of from my childhood.

My heart fluttered thinking about these iconic, yet overproduced pieces of cardboard. Whether it was the 1990 Leaf Frank Thomas, the 1987 Topps card featuring the 75 pound Barry Bonds or even the 1990 Score Bo Jackson, it was all so intriguing to build my very own complete library of all the cards from my childhood. I always had this vision of putting all the sets in binders so I could enjoy them anytime I wanted. I blame this largely on an image from an old issue of Beckett magazine when I was a child.

I vividly remember the picture of a child about my age sitting with his legs crossed in the middle of his clean room. In his lap was a nice binder that housed a complete set of 1983 Topps. As if that wasn't enough to make any 12-year-old baseball card collecting child jealous, you could look up further in the picture to see a bookshelf filled with perfectly uniform baseball card albums, all neatly labeled with what they had in them. I don't recall anything else about why the picture was there, but the caption of the picture may as well have read *"Little Tommy is sitting in his bedroom looking at his cards while reveling in the fact that he is richer than you, and also has a better collection than you do."*

**Junk Wax:
A Gateway Drug**

Did You Know?

If placed top to bottom, the alleged entire print run of 1991 Topps baseball cards could go all the way around the world ... seven times!

To say this hobby has evolved is an understatement. The mass-produced cardboard of old acted as a gateway drug for me to see what else was available. As everyone knows, the internet changed the hobby dramatically. The cards that were hot back in the 80s and 90s may still be desirable, but now only go for a small fraction of what they used to. A good example would be a 1989 Donruss Ken Griffey Jr. Griffey has always been loved. (Are there any baseball fans who don't like him?) He has always been heavily collected, and in his playing days before the advent of the internet, his rookie cards would command a premium.

Once eBay started, dealers were delighted to reach a whole new audience with ease. They could put up a 1989 Donruss Griffey for $10 and access countless potential buyers. The problem? They were now competing with countless other dealers (and collectors!) trying to sell for $10 as well. Some would even sell them in lots of 10 or more. Eventually, you could easily find Griffey's precious rated rookie for a sliver of what the price guides were reporting.

Keep in mind that this was for what previously was considered to be a hot card. Many others from this time period are now nearly worthless. A quick eBay search for "1989 Griffey" shows nearly 6,250 listings that have been sold over the past three months - and that doesn't even take into account the several listings that have multiple Griffey rookies.

The market on the 80s and 90s stuff has dropped like a rock for almost everything across the board. The internet revealed one thing to collectors: there were significantly more cards that were produced than anyone could have ever imagined. For many of us, our beloved hobby started in the junk wax era – the mid to late '80s until the early to mid-'90s. It is from this time period which all other collecting periods are measured, and unfairly so.

"The hobby isn't what it used to be" everyone cries out, remembering when card shops could be found at every corner, and packs of cards could be purchased everywhere from candy stores to petting zoos. Why do so many people say these cards are better used as firewood than anything else? The answer is simple: the card companies seemingly kept the presses running for eternity.

When 1991 Topps came out, everyone was excited about the promotion they were running. Topps randomly inserted buybacks and buyback redemptions for one of every card they released from the past 40 years in their packs. If my math is right, that means over 25,000 cards and redemptions were inserted. That would make anyone think they had a decent shot at pulling one, but it has been said that they printed an estimated four to five million copies of every single 1991 Topps baseball card. If these numbers are true, that means that it wouldn't take several boxes to pull one, but several cases. Imagine how frustrating it would be if you made it your mission to pull one of these randomly inserted cards, and after opening seven cases, your prize was a 1988 Topps Nick Esasky!

Don't think for a moment that such gaudy numbers were exclusive to 1991 Topps, either. Virtually all cards from the junk wax era were heavily produced by all companies. In a sense, the sheer volume of cards printed from this era has helped collectors get back into collecting at a very affordable point of entry. When complete sets and wax boxes from your childhood can be picked up for a fraction of what they used to sell for, and you were buying them as a child when you were making a fraction of what you are now, it is easy to justify slipping into a couple wax boxes of 1990 Donruss or 1989 Fleer.

Somewhere along the way, something happened to me, much like what has happened to many former childhood collecting adults. Using this cheap gateway drug that we shall affectionately call cardboard crack, got us back into the hobby thinking "Boy, these new cards sure are fancy! Maybe I'll pick up a pack or two." It is all downhill from there.

DECRYPTING THE NOSTALGIA CONNECTION

So, how does this connection happen? How is it, that our love for 1988 Score turned into an addiction for expensive bat knob cards that don't look or feel anything like the cards of our youth? Junk wax is truly a cheap gateway drug. When you see the newer eye candy, it is exciting. A chrome card here, an unnumbered auto there. The next thing you know, you are looking for cards serial numbered to 10 or less and battling it out with other collectors every step of the way.

The "friction" created by your competition makes you feel like each rare card you purchase at auction or otherwise is a trophy for winning it. The fact that other collectors want the cards you have won goes a long way in validating your obsession. It makes you feel like you have something truly desirable that was worth all of the effort you made to secure it in your collection.

There is also something to be said about the online collecting community as a whole, too. When you talk about baseball cards in public nowadays, people will act as if they just heard you confess to playing with My Little Pony dolls as an adult. This isn't the '80s anymore – people just aren't chatting it up about cardboard as they used to in person. When you go online, you can find countless like-minded collectors all showing off their newest acquisitions and passionately telling stories that go along with them.

It is infectious! A virtual community is formed, and everyone encourages each other to purchase more cards continuously. Not only do you have the excitement of winning a card over your competition; you are also given an endless flow of compliments for your recent purchases, which breeds more drive and all the validation you need to continue getting more cards.

Confessions of a Baseball Card Addict

Perhaps one of the last pieces of the puzzle to understanding how it is we as collectors make the jump from the cardboard of our youth to today's high-end cards is the fact that the Internet makes it an endless treasure hunt. When we were younger, we would bring our want lists to card shows, shops and trading sessions with our friends. Beyond that, we didn't really have any other options.

Because we can now go on an unending virtual excursion for what we want, there is no end in sight. Just because something isn't on eBay today doesn't mean it won't be there tomorrow. If it isn't there tomorrow, it may be somewhere else on the internet.

OBSESSED WITH LITTLE SQUARE PIECES OF FABRIC

While I rediscovered my love for the cardboard of my childhood, something else caught my eye. During my absence from the hobby, eBay made it quite apparent that I had missed out on a tremendously large assortment of innovative cards. It was almost as if I had gotten out right when things were starting to get interesting. There were now some really nice reflective cards, die-cut inserts and tons of serial numbered cards. My mom and dad bought a box of 2006 Future Stars for my birthday one year - not because I asked for cards, but because they thought it would be a fun throwback gift to the days of my childhood.

One of the cards I pulled was an Alex Rodriguez card numbered to 99. I seriously thought I had a big money card because I knew A-Rod was a big deal. The serial numbering made it extra special to me. How on earth was I so lucky to land one where only 98 others were out there? When I was a child, some cards would be numbered to 10,000, and they were impossible to find. Little did I know that cards numbered to 99 nowadays were common, and not really considered special.

Perhaps the cards that really got my heart racing were the "game-used" cards. I can't really describe the affection I had for them in any other way than it being a true obsession. These cards were something I had never heard about before in my life.

In an effort to take card collecting to the next level and pump up sales, card companies would take game-used bats and jerseys, then chop them up into little pieces to embed them in cards. To the card collecting community, this was the biggest thing to happen to the hobby in a long time, and it was exactly what the hobby needed. To own a baseball card of your favorite player that has a 3/4" square piece of fabric worn by him in a major league baseball game felt special. To rub your finger on the jersey piece and feel the material would give you a personal connection to the game and the player - all for a few dollars.

I found this new innovation to be quite an ironic way to lure old collectors back in again because whenever I would ask people why they left the hobby, they would typically say because there were simply too many types of gimmicky cards being produced.

While collecting one of every set was still something I was interested in, I couldn't help but jump onto the game-used bandwagon head first. Boy, did I ever. To make things even more interesting for collectors, card companies were even inserting autographed cards into packs - with a certificate of authenticity note on the card itself! These autographs always seemed so perfect and uniform. The design of the card would typically have a spot for the autograph, which was always signed using the proper pen or marker.

While IP/TTM (In Person / Through the Mail) autographs still thrive today, they are typically never able to aesthetically compete with pack-pulled, on-card autographs. Aside from the fact that IP/TTM autographs could be signed in a wide array of low-quality pens & markers, the cards you get signed won't have a place specifically for a signature, nor will you get a COA.

AUTOGRAPHS AND PARALLELS GALORE

Gone are the days of being satisfied with just one autograph of your favorite player. I remember reading about one Ken Griffey Jr. collector in Beckett who had three of his autographs. My first though was why would he need more than one autograph? Isn't that overkill? As it turns out, he was just ahead of his time.

At the time of this writing, Shohei Ohtani has only played in just over 100 baseball games, yet has nearly 700 autographed baseball cards. Ohtani has almost seven times as many autographed cards than games he has played in at the major league level! An extreme amount of autographed cards for just about any star player can be found nowadays too, and collectors want as many of them as they can get their hands on.

Card companies have taken notice that collectors are willing to pony up big cash for cards with the tiniest of differences. Because of this, they will create the same card, along with five, ten or even twenty variations. Many of these also have autographed parallels, as well. Oftentimes, the differences between each variation is a simple serial number and border color change.

From the outside looking in, all of these autographs and parallels may sound ludicrous, but the market is there for them. Card companies have taken a lot of heat for producing so many different variations, but not capitalizing on the situation would be a poor business decision for any company.

COLLECTING AIMLESSLY, AND LOSING FOCUS

Once I learned of game-used and autographed cards, I started buying them up like crazy, paying between $1-5 each for them as if I had struck gold. I ended up with hundreds of them, without rhyme or reason. Anything from a Jason Giambi bat card to a Mark Kotsay autograph, I was after anything I could get my hands on.

In a short period of time, I had dropped a couple of thousand dollars on these random game-used & autographed cards and found myself feeling very uncomfortable. At the same time, I was picking up the complete sets from my youth as well, so I was out a sizeable amount of money within a couple of months of re-entering the seemingly harmless, cheap hobby from my youth. Something had to be done. The complete sets were not really "doing it" for me just sitting in the closet. It would be fun knowing that I had most of the cards I had fawned over from my youth, but looking at them didn't really get me excited. Just like I did as a child, I stacked the sets on top of each other in my closet so that I could see the ends of each one.

The bright graphics from a 1989 Fleer factory set sat right on top of a plain brown 1988 Donruss factory set, which sat next to a hand collated set of 1990 Score that had its name handwritten in black marker directly on the box with its previous price scribbled out. The presentation was simply not very appealing and no longer inspired me to continue on with my goal. My dream of putting the sets in binders just like I saw had been done in Beckett years ago faded. Loaded up with countless junk wax era sets and a large hoard of meaningless game-used & autographed cards, I decided once again to call it quits.

SELLING OUT

I didn't like how my hobby was costing me so much money and taking up so much space. I decided to sell off everything I had from my childhood as well as my recent obsessive purchases, aside from my beloved Canseco card collection. The number cruncher in me broke out Microsoft Excel, and I started documenting every single card & set I had purchased, to determine how much of a loss I was going to take from selling off what I had amassed. This was a daunting task, as

I wasn't originally purchasing to sell, so I felt that this exercise, though necessary, would set myself up for disappointment.

I kicked into hustle mode and started selling things off bit by bit. Craigslist was flooded with listings of my complete sets, game-used lots, team sets and more. My spreadsheet would show the list of my cards and purchase prices, as well as all the sales I would make. It was fun to see the average price I paid per game-used / auto card drop from $2 to $1.75 to $1.25 after having sold several of them. Within a short amount of time, the amount I had into each card continued to drop and averaged out to be .75 cents, then .50 cents. Eventually, I ended up making all of my money back - and had a lot of cards left over. Something clicked in me. Because of my buying and selling, I had a lot of game-used & autograph cards that were essentially free!

Slowly, but surely, all of my complete sets, vintage and newer singles were sold off as well. I had a feeling of accomplishment - that I was able to once again make money from the hobby I had loved as a child. Perhaps this was the feeling I was chasing all along. The ability to be in the hobby without it being a financial drain, and make money while doing it. It is awesome to own a box of nice cards that cost me absolutely nothing after selling the others for profit!

This really got me to re-thinking my exodus of the hobby. Do I really want to get out? If I'm making money with them and having a blast doing it, why should I stop buying cards? Heck, I made money on cards I didn't think I was going to be able to, so I wonder how well I could do if I started purchasing with the intent to sell? I decided to go this direction, but this time with profit in mind as well as enjoyment. I'm glad I decided this because it has been a fun ride over the past several years.

VISITING THE CARD SHOP OF MY YOUTH

Around this time, I took my family on a road trip to visit my parents over 2,000 miles away to my hometown Fresno,

California. One of the things I wanted to do was to stop by my favorite childhood place: The Bullpen. It had been closed down for a few years, but to my surprise had re-opened in a new location. I walked in the shop, and the owner Mike - my childhood hero - remembered me after all those years!

I was able to introduce him to Holly and Atticus, which was great to be able to do nearly two decades after the first time I stepped foot in his shop. We spent a long time talking to him about collecting. I had asked him what he had for sale, and just like he would do when I was a child, he brought a bunch of cards out from the back to show me. I was able to walk away with a number of boxes filled with superstars and several classic sets. Before we left, Holly took a picture of him with Atticus and me. It was a great memory!

When we got back to my parent's house, I shuffled through the cards and laid them out just like I would do as a child. It was heaven! There were multiples of 1998 Topps Mark McGwire, 1997 Pinnacle Frank Thomas, 1996 Donruss Ken Griffey Jr. and 1995 Score Barry Bonds, to name a few. Many of them were from my "lost years" of collecting - the mid-'90s. Though many of the cards were worth no more than a quarter each, it was truly enjoyable to see cards I had never seen of players that I grew up watching.

When we returned home, I started religiously looking online for deals to be had. I would tirelessly look for people selling their collections and dealers selling their inventories. The majority of people I ran across were trying to sell thousands of commons from 1988-1992 as if they were gold. It was rare to find an amazing collection or inventory amongst countless junk listings, but finding a diamond in the rough was my new obsession.

Cardboard Alchemy

Did You Know?

If you are lucky enough to own a 1956 Topps Hank
Aaron, you have two Hall of Famers for the price
of one. While the headshot is Hank Aaron, the action
shot is actually Willie Mays.

Not much could beat the feeling of purchasing a collection with a 1993 SP Jeter rookie, selling the collection and having the Jeter for free, along with a pile of cash. It made me feel like Rumpelstiltskin. This was the game I played, and the rules of my game were simple:

- Buy a collection
- Have fun going through the cards
- Take out the cards I wanted to keep & sell the rest
- Make money and have cards left over for free

This was the true meaning of "for fun and profit" to me, and is what I consider cardboard alchemy. Sure, a lot of time and effort was involved, but when you love something like I love baseball cards, it doesn't seem like work at all.

I have come across some incredible items, but no matter what it was, I would always see more value in the money than the item. It didn't mean that I didn't love the pieces; I just never really came across anything that I had a desire to keep, until I began my Canseco Supercollecting journey several years later.

Through all this, I realized that I was not just a collector, but also a dealer. Not only a dealer; but a dealer who was buying out dealers. Over the course of a decade, I dealt in excess of ten million cards.

I purchased collections that would fill my minivan and inventories that would fill my garage. Armed with an outlet to share my dealing experiences through my blog, the feedback from my audience motivated me further to look for deals. Listed below are a few of them that have stood out to me over the years.

THE CASE OF THE 18 CASES

One of my earliest "scores" as a dealer came from someone locally. I found someone that mentioned they had a bunch of unopened cases of baseball cards for sale from their shop they had closed down several years prior. The majority were from 1989 to 1992, but it looked very intriguing. I reached out, and the ex-dealer sent me a spreadsheet of everything he had. Aside from the cases of baseball cards, he had several football and basketball cases as well. This was a little out of my comfort zone as I was just getting into buying cards to resell for profit, so I decided to contact him about his baseball cases.

After going back and forth for a while, we ultimately came to an agreement. For $400, I was the proud owner of 18 cases of baseball cards - and he delivered them to me! I was not used to spending this kind of money on baseball cards in one shot, but at roughly $20 a sealed case, it seemed to make sense. All 18 cases sat in our living room for longer than Holly would have liked. For some reason, she doesn't share the same love for baseball cards that I have.

There were cases of 1989 Fleer, 1990 Upper Deck, 1992 Topps, and various others. The one thing I wanted so badly as a child was to be able to open a full case of baseball cards and now I had 18 taking up a considerable amount of space in our house. It would literally keep me up at night as a child. The thought of busting through 20 solid boxes of 1989 Score was the stuff my dreams were made of. This was like heaven, but it got even better.

As we were loading up the last case in my living room, he put it down on the ground and said "Oh yeah, one more thing - I was wrong. This isn't a case of 1990 Upper Deck complete sets. It is a case of 1989 Upper Deck complete sets." That is like buying a car, and the sales guy saying "Here are the keys to your Honda, sir. Oh, by the way - it is actually a Corvette."

This made an already sweet deal absolutely ridiculous! I ended up making all my money back and then some by just selling that one case to somebody's girlfriend in Seattle. She thought it would make an excellent gift for her boyfriend who was a Griffey fan. Not much longer after that, someone else contacted me. A little league coach who wanted to buy all the commons from a case of 1992 Topps. This allowed me to break my first case ever, but on someone else's dime, and keep all the goodies. With 20 boxes of 36 packs each, I busted 720 packs and had a blast doing it!

Not long after this, I was contacted by a nice older man who buys cards on the cheap to have fun going through them and then give the rest away to sick or poor children. Because of this, I agreed to sell to him for less than I had originally wanted. In the end, I made some profit, fulfilled my lifelong dream of opening a full case and Holly got our living room back inside of about three weeks.

THE ESTATE SALE FIND

A little over a month later, I was searching online for deals and came upon an estate sale. Among a myriad of items listed for sale was a line that simply said "baseball cards". I emailed and asked them if they could elaborate. Their response was short. *"We are unable to give you any information about them. If you are interested, please drive out here tomorrow morning before 12 and take a look for yourself."*

It was a good 45-minute drive, and I don't even know why I bothered, because the odds were it was just going to be a pile of 1988 Score bound together by rubber bands. Ultimately, I decided to drive out and take a look because it was Saturday morning and it would be a perfect time to check out something like this. I was expecting a house, but it ended up being an apartment. People were buzzing in and out of this person's home, carrying armloads of things back to their cars.

The owner was an older gentleman who could no longer live on his own anymore, so his family flew out from California to sell his belongings and take him back with them. As I walked in, I told a woman that I was the one who emailed about the baseball cards. She led me into a separate room where there were thick matching binders filled with baseball cards wall to wall - 75 of them in all.

When I dug in, I quickly found out that the man had taken all of his baseball cards and placed all players in order by their last name. Some letters had multiple binders represented. When you look at a collection organized this way, you don't start with "A". You start with "G" for Griffey or "J" for Jeter. I went to the "G" binder first to see if anything good was in it, and as I opened the binder, it was as if there was no real rhyme or reason as to how they were placed in the pages. The pages had all kinds of different years and brands of different players. I was beginning to think the man had more money in the binders and pages than the actual cards themselves. 1991 Fleer, 1995 Score Select, 1994 SP, and others could be found.

After flipping through several pages with nothing but commons to show, there were some Griffey rookies and game-used cards randomly throughout the binder. I went to "R" for Ripken & Rodriguez, and it was the same. Then "J" for Jeter and "T" for Thomas. While I knew the bulk of the collection would be commons, I just wanted to make sure all the good stuff wasn't taken out already. There was enough to justify making a move. The woman came in to check on me, and I gave her an offer of $400 for everything. She didn't like that too terribly much, and I said the highest I would be willing to go was $450.

"Well, a man came in and offered $500. He said he would come back for them if I agreed to the price, but I like you more, so I'll accept your offer for $450."

I gave her the money, and she helped me make several trips back & forth to load my car to the brim with binders. When I got home to take a closer look, I was delighted to see that there were TONS of star rookies and game-used/autographed cards throughout the binders! I had a blast going through everything over the next few weeks, and ended up selling the cards with all the low-end stuff in it for more than I paid for the entire collection - plus, I had an enormous amount of good cards left over for free.

At the time of purchase, I calculated that I had about $6 in each binder, which I figured when you factored in the pages as well, it was a good price even if no cards at all came along with the deal. I was even able to keep several binders and pages for my own personal stockpile. It seemed like a number of collections I purchased would include lots of new storage supplies, so for a long time, I never needed to buy any.

The entire room worth of binders sat in my office and stayed there while I would spend the next several days enjoying going through and listing them. The only downside was that it made my office smell like a 90-year-old had lived there. A small price to pay for living amidst cardboard gold!

Over the next several months, I made several deals of various sizes. It was pure bliss. I was truly enjoying myself with the thrill of the hunt. One issue I always seemed to run into was the challenge of educating the seller on the value of their cards. Everyone heard stories from their parents about how they had all kinds of cards in the attic from the '50s that were worth a small fortune. Because of this, many thought that their collection of '80s cards would be worth something as well. As a buyer, I had to break the news to them that many of their cards were virtually worthless. Some would be accepting of this and others would walk off in a huff. I was able to fine tune my "speech" somewhat so I could sound as convincing as possible, without being offensive. Many of these deals were for $50-$200 early on. The next deal, however, is one that I'll remember forever.

THE SIX MILLION CARD DEAL

Before I went into selling mode, I met someone online who worked as a part-time dealer since 1985. Not only did Dwain set up at card shows, he also used to promote them. I first reached out to him when I was still trying to collect one of every complete set from the '80s and early '90s. He said he had some, and invited me over to his house. When I got there, he had about six complete sets sitting on his dining room table. I was underwhelmed because I thought he had a lot to choose from. I was very disappointed, and don't even recall buying any from him that day. Then he showed me his garage.

As he pulled up the garage door, it was a different story. I am fairly certain I heard angels singing. 800 count boxes were stacked floor to ceiling as if they were massive Jenga structures. Countless 2,700, 3,200 and 5,000 card boxes were housed there as well. The cards in the garage were situated in rows and columns, front to back, spaced out with just enough room for a person to get through them. I was speechless. Unfortunately, he didn't have anything else to sell me at that time, but I knew he would at some point - he also mentioned that he had a few storage units packed with cards as well.

Over the next several months, Dwain and I became friends, and I purchased a lot of cards from him. Sometimes in bulk of 100,000 at a time. It was a blast being able to go through them all, and I frequently went back to him for more. One day, I had him over to show him what I had. As we sat in the very office that I am writing this, I showed him a number of signed jerseys & bats that I had recently purchased, as well as a ton of stars, rookies & inserts I acquired from various collections. After going back and forth, we ended up making a deal: All my "good" stuff for six million of his cards.

I received a lot of negative feedback from others saying it was a horrible deal, but I knew what I was doing. The deal worked out great, as he agreed to bring them over a little at a time, so that way I didn't have to store all those cards in my house. I don't even think my house could store that many unless we wanted to use the cards as furniture.

I would refer to Dwain as Santa Claus because he would always come over with a vehicle packed full of cardboard for me. Though the deal happened years ago, I still have over two million cards left to go through. This has been one of the most fun deals I have made, and I always enjoy watching people's eyes bulge when I tell them how many cards were involved!

MASSIVE WAX PACK FIND

I have picked up a number of collections under many peculiar circumstances. One collection I picked up due to someone needing money to bail someone from jail. Another had a run of complete sets from Topps dating back to the early '80s that were purchased as an investment with the intent to put them through college. The entire run ended up being picked up for under $90. There are countless other stories I have, but this next story comes from a guy whose father passed away. He was called to remove his belongings from his father's home. When he got there, he found a ton of recent unopened wax packs.

This person posted an ad online stating that he had a bunch of wax packs that he would sell for 50 cents each. While I was expecting the pictures to show a bunch of 1990 Upper Deck and 1988 Fleer, I was pleasantly surprised. All of the packs were 2009 and newer. There were tons of Allen & Ginter, Heritage, Platinum and more. I hastily emailed him asking when we could meet, and he said the next morning. I was so excited, I could barely sleep! He was nearly an hour away, but if what he was saying was true, it would be well worth the trip.

The next morning, I got up early and made the drive. I was just down the street from the seller when I received an email saying that he could not meet anymore. Something had come up, and maybe later would work. I decided to email him asking for a different time/day. Crickets. I waited all day and didn't hear a peep. I emailed him again and still nothing. Had I come on too strong? Did I sound like stranger danger? I wasn't exactly sure what the problem was, but I knew I couldn't just give up. At the same time, I didn't want to be annoying and pester him. I did the next logical thing and contacted him using an alias account.

Let me start by saying that I do not condone this sort of activity. It was not my intention to be deceitful. I just wanted to see if he was ignoring me. My fake identity was to approach him in a much more laid-back manner. If he responded to my fake account and not my real one, I knew that I would have no chance of using my real account to set up something with him again.

As I crafted an email to him, I casually asked questions about the collection. Much to my surprise, he responded quickly. I was astonished. What on earth could I have said under my real account that would have made him feel so uncomfortable? In any event, he was comfortable with the fake me coming over to his apartment, so it worked out. I drove up there once more and knocked on the door. The man opened up the door to his small upstairs apartment. His entire front room was covered in loose packs of sports cards. The majority were baseball, but there were some football and basketball as well.

It was almost as if 25 sports card sections at Walmart had exploded in his living room! The only thing I wanted to do was pull a Scrooge McDuck and swim in them. I asked if anyone had purchased any yet, and he told me someone came the day before to buy 100 packs for $50. I was fine with that because that wasn't even the tip of the iceberg. The seller said the plan was just to keep selling them at 50 cents a pack, so I asked what he would be willing to take for everything. We went back and forth for a while, and I even found that he had several binders full of great cards as well. We came to a price of $420. I loaded up everything (while almost blowing my cover by saying my real name when I was retelling a story to him!) and drove off. I'm telling you, I am not cut out for living a double life!

When I got home, I quickly unloaded and started counting the packs. There ended up being around 5,700 in total. I had no idea there were that many, so I was very excited. Over the next several months, I enjoyed them by opening nearly every single pack myself. It would be a fun ritual of mine each day to grab a pile of packs to open at my desk, or while watching a baseball game. In addition to having fun ripping all of them, I was also able to sell what I opened for a nice profit.

BLACK FRIDAY

When you think of Black Friday, you may think of good deals and mass chaos. I think about news stories of people being trampled to death in the name of finding a killer deal on a flat screen television. If there is one thing I know about this wretched day, it is that I will not venture out in public for anything. This suits me just fine though because the largest online baseball card dealers run specials, which meant that I would stay chained to my desk.

For a handful of years on Black Friday, I would set my alarm at 4 am, grab some breakfast and a caffeinated beverage, then wear out the refresh button on my keyboard to see what new special was going to pop up next on the Blowout Cards website. I imagine this was the same for countless other collectors looking to score a good deal, as multiple cases of cards would sell out in seconds. I always seemed to do well, though. I would sometimes end up spending several thousand dollars to pick up these cases and sell them locally throughout the year.

Doing this was a fun way to deal in wax and break some boxes for free at the same time. Finding ways to make money off of lots like this was like a fun puzzle for me to figure out and was truly rewarding. The only downside was looking back at what I sold, and seeing that I had dozens of boxes of 2011 Topps Update for $40 each which routinely go for nearly ten times that now!

THE TRI-STAR BASEBALL CARD SHOW

Twice a year, the Tri-Star baseball card show would come into town. This is the same show where I first met Jose Canseco when I was a child. I am not exaggerating when I say it felt like Christmas to me every time I attended. I would be among the first to show up on Friday, and among the last to leave on Sunday. Atticus would come with me at least once each year, and we would have a ritual of partaking in a ridiculously overpriced hot dog, soda and hunk of fudge. It was a fun bonding time for us. While he was more in it for the junk food, it was fun to be able to explain to him what was significant about the T206 cards and Babe Ruth signatures. From time to time, we would run into Star Wars figures or cards, and his eyes would light up.

I would go from table to table looking for deals I could make money on. I could frequently be seen borrowing a dealer's dolly to wheel out newly purchased inventories to my minivan, which I affectionately call the cardboard mobile. While it was good to be there early to get the hot stuff, it was even better to be there at the end. You could catch dealers looking to unload their tables of stuff they were unable to sell.

Many times, what I found is that I could sell the bulk of stuff that the dealers couldn't. I would try my best to sharpshoot what I thought I could move for a good enough profit, and oftentimes, that meant going for things in bulk. Whether it was 200 complete sets of junk wax, a hoard of framed autograph pictures, a Pete Rose autographed bat lot or boxes of vintage commons. If it was something I thought I could move, I would pick it up. Some of the greatest times for me would be sticking around at the end of the show and buying out a dealer's entire multi-table setup.

7,000+ AUTOGRAPHED BASEBALL CARD DEAL

One day while I was browsing listings on eBay, I noticed someone selling some "in person" (IP) autographed baseball cards in lots of 50 for cheap. I reached out to him and asked if that was all he had, or if he had anything more. As it turned out, the seller had over 7,000 autographed cards. Going to various Spring Training and baseball games was his life for 20 years. I considered making an offer on the entire collection, but it was difficult to do something like that, sight unseen.

I told him my plans and asked to purchase a small sample lot of 200 or so autographs, so I could get a better feel for what he had. We ended up striking a deal: All of his autographs for $1,300. At the price I paid, I knew I could buy everything and turn a nice profit, with a little work. Before doing so though, I wanted to make sure they were from a smoke-free home, that most autographs were from major leaguers and that there weren't dozens of autographed cards of the same player over and over again. It is one thing to sell 40 New York Yankees common autographed cards. It is quite another if the 40 Yankees cards are all Andy Stankiewicz.

I was nervous for them to come in because you never know what could happen to cards in transit. Did he just ship in a few 3,200 count boxes? What if they were dropped en-route and the corners of an entire row of cards were dinged? The cards ended up making it over just fine, and quite frankly were overwhelming. What was I going to do with 7,000+ autographed cards? My first thought was to pull the good ones and list them to recoup my money as quickly as possible. Another idea I had was to put them in team lots, though it would have taken a lot of work to organize. Ultimately, after selling a few small amounts of them, I ended up putting them online for sale as one large collection.

Within three weeks of purchasing, I had a bite. A dealer and his partner messaged me, asking the usual questions. You know the questions - if they were from a smoke-free home, mostly major leaguers and if they were all Andy Stankiewicz. I told them yes, yes and no. That was enough for them, so they ended up doing the deal with me and flew from out of state to come and check them out. After about an hour or so of going through them, they bought the lot for $3,500 and were on their way.

A MASSIVE HAUL OF ... COMIC BOOKS?

I never really was a comic book nerd. Sure, as a kid, I had some, but it never really was an obsession of mine. I loved Spiderman, Punisher and remember when the comics came out about Superman being dead. One day in 2012, while I was checking out what was for sale on Craigslist, I found a guy who was selling his comic book collection for $600. This was intriguing to me, so I made the drive out to see them.

I had no idea what I was looking at, so I had to reach out to my dealer friend Dwain, whom I did the six million card deal with (he is a huge comic book collector), and he said at that price, it seemed to be a safe bet. There were 24 long boxes, so it came out to be less than $17 a box, which was a no-brainer for me. After recouping nearly all of my initial investment by selling to collectors locally, I sold everything else for a $1,200 profit by shipping them to a shop in Dallas inside of three weeks.

When it rains, it pours, right? Over the next year and a half, I ended up acquiring about five different large comic book collections of all shapes and sizes. With how much I hated the idea of having a minivan years ago, I can't tell you how happy I was to have one during all my various purchasing excursions.

A few months later, I reached out to a lady who was selling her comic books. She mentioned she had tons of long boxes filled with DC comics that were all bagged and boarded.

I made her an offer of $800, and she said no because she had a better deal out there. It turned out the guy she was talking about was the same person that left me hanging on a deal for my previous comic lot I had just sold, so I had a sneaking suspicion that he would do the same to her. I thanked her for her time, requested she keep my phone number and waited to hear back from her.

Exactly a month from the time I bought the other collection, I received a text from her:

"You can pick up the collection now if you still want it." My suspicions were correct! The guy that bailed on me, ended up bailing on her too, and she said she had to get them out of her house because she was moving. After dinner and going through our routine with Atticus at night for bedtime, I armed myself with some caffeine, an MxPx CD, and set out for the drive that was over an hour away.

After speaking with her for a while, it turns out it was her recently deceased husband's collection. He had passed away earlier in the year. I felt horrible for her, so needless to say, I wasn't in full bargaining mode - even though there were fewer comics than I expected. While the deal ended up working out great, the worst part was probably bringing them all from her upstairs room to the cardboard … err … comic book mobile. I was able to move the collection fairly quickly, and then it happened again. More comics!

Each time I would sell a comic collection, it would be right on the heels of making a deal for another comic collection. The same day I sold the comics of the lady's deceased husband, I started talking to someone else about his collection. I told him I was ready to buy, and he said he was holding them for someone who put a deposit on them and took a third of the collection with him. Throughout the next few weeks, I checked in, and he still said he was waiting, but the deadline was set for December 3rd.

If the guy didn't come up with the cash, he was going to allow me to come over. I was excited, though, at this point, I had forgotten what kind of deal it was. I just remembered it was a killer deal.

I asked him to remind me, and it turned out to be the same amount of comics from the last deal (about 7,000) for $400. I was just hoping that the other guy would bail out, and he did! Friday night, I made the half hour trek up to his house. It was amazing. He told me I probably had three or four trips to make, but I assured him my minivan had an incredible amount of room in it, and has handled 7,000 comics with ease before.

As I walked in his house, I was guided to a room in the back that was stuffed to the gills with comic books! There was no way this was only 7,000. I loaded up the minivan to the brim, and there were so many more to go. I asked if I could unload them at home and come back. He agreed, and I must say, I had the most miserable time unloading them. It was past midnight, and I was exhausted. On the bright side, the total count was approximately 20,000 comics. I had never seen that many or had that many comics before at one time. It took two trips, and I was praying all the way home that the clearance between the back tires and wheel wells would still be there.

I was in absolute shock. There were many duplicates, and it was so overwhelming, I didn't even know where or how to begin looking. It is one thing to have 20,000 baseball cards in your garage. It is quite another when you have 20,000 comic books. That many cards would take up a tiny corner of my garage, but that many comic books would take up the majority of my entire garage.

Thankfully it didn't take long for someone slightly crazier than me to make the purchase for $3,000. The buyer told me he had a warehouse where he stored all of his treasures away from his wife so she wouldn't know anything about his purchasing habits. Boy, is she going to be surprised if he passes away before she does! On the day of the sale, he hired a team of three guys with a massive 18 wheeler to load up everything and drive off. It was always satisfying to see a fairly empty garage after being packed up to the ceiling for a while.

WHEN THE HOLDERS ARE WORTH MORE THAN THE CARDS

One day, I responded to an ad for a 400,000 baseball card collection. I reached out to the owner, and he said I could come over in the evening. I made the trip over and immediately knew the guy was doing well for himself. The neighborhood I entered to get to him was very upscale. His house looked like a mansion. He came out and had me meet him in his garage, where he had a beautiful flat screen television with a football game on. The garage was oversized, and parked in the left of it was a beautiful brand new Corvette. The more I got to speak with him, the more evident it was that he had been partaking in a number of alcoholic beverages. He wasn't slurring his speech or falling over, but he smelled of alcohol and seemed very chatty.

He mentioned to me that he purchased everything from a dealer about 11 years ago, who passed away due to cancer. He had $15,000 into the entire inventory. It was obvious he had sold many of the original cards before I got my paws on them as there simply wasn't nearly $15,000 worth in the lot (or perhaps he severely overpaid) but still, there were many fantastic cards. There were hundreds of autographs and several brand new heavy duty tubs filled with memorabilia.

Before making an offer, I asked him if this was all of the collection. His eyes darted around for a while and said *"Oh yeah! Wait a minute."* He hopped inside and came back out with another few piles of cards - these cards ended up being the best in the entire bunch. Remember, kids - ALWAYS ask if that is all they have! I made an offer, and he accepted $1,300 for everything. Well, everything that he wasn't still hiding in his house.

As with any collection, this one came with thousands upon thousands of junk wax commons. Instead of cardboard boxes though, they were in these plastic two-row containers. This was probably the biggest surprise of all in the collection. Just for the heck of it, I checked online to see what the containers themselves were going for. As it turned out, the containers were worth much more than the common cards themselves. I was able to make hundreds of dollars selling them off and dumping the cards into cardboard boxes. When the dust had settled, I sold everything for $4,600.

THE MILLION CARD INVENTORY

The largest deal I ever made (that required me to take on the entire inventory all at once) was from a dealer who decided to get out of the business. He stated he had over a million cards. I am generally skeptical of these kinds of phone calls. I've had several of them in the past, and they never quite seem to be what they are supposed to be. Whenever I go to check them out, they typically seem to be a small fraction of the quantity they state, and almost always tend to be filled with 1988 Donruss Greg Jefferies, 1990 Upper Deck Eric Anthony, or similar.

I drove out to his residence, and it was not looking good. Across the street was a house that had suffered massive fire damage, and the house I was going to appeared to be all of 800 square feet at best, with the roof caving in. There was a thought in my mind to just drive on by. The odds of anything decent being there were slim, but this is a case of not judging a book by its cover. I chose to hop out and knock on the door. I did, after all, drive 45 minutes for this - I might as well take a peek!

A nice older gentleman opened the door and explained he needed to get out of the house because the landlord wasn't properly taking care of it. The cards were just too much to move.

Confessions of a Baseball Card Addict

He guided me to a room where monster boxes were piled from floor to ceiling, wall to wall. Everything was situated on heavy duty shelving units. It was right then and there that I believed this might be the real deal. Every box was properly titled, and nearly all the cards were in order! It was difficult to believe that one person could do all of this sorting in one lifetime.

He then led me to the 2nd room. This room had a bed and a television... and more monster boxes lining the walls that were stacked floor to ceiling. As we made our way to the front room, there were long boxes stuffed under light stands, smaller boxes in a curio cabinet and other boxes on the floor. Walking further into the house to the kitchen was truly a sight to see. The nook that was meant for a refrigerator was filled with - you guessed it - baseball cards. Even the carport *outside* was loaded up with cards! At least a tarp was over them.

Simply put, I had never seen anything quite like this before in my entire life. I don't know what was more jaw-dropping: The fact that this man lived in a cardboard palace or that every card was in order. Every nook and cranny had cardboard, and there was so much of it, that it was even spilling out to his driveway. He could have been a legitimate candidate to be on one of the television hoarding shows.

On the phone, he mentioned it would take $1,000 to get everything. When I told him I would take it and proceeded to give him the $1,000, he balked saying it wouldn't be $1,000 for everything. It would be $2,000. It is never fun to have someone pull a bait and switch on you after having driven a long ways away. Perhaps he was second guessing his decision to sell, but even at double the quoted price, I was still a buyer. Thankfully, I brought more money with me just in case, so I gave it to him as quickly as possible, before he could change his mind.

I made four trips across town loading up the cardboard mobile to the gills, testing its suspension to the limits each time.

All told, it was six hours of drive time alone, not to mention the countless hours of loading & unloading. Fortunately, every last card (barely) fit in my garage. Over the course of the next three months, I enjoyed hanging out in the garage just to look through some of them. It was a blast!

It would have been impossible to go through everything in a lifetime, but since every box was labeled, I was able to take a look at the boxes that interested me. The curiosity could have easily killed me. I remember making my best impression of Dig Dug, by lifting boxes and putting them behind me over and over again just to see what was in the middle of literally tons of cardboard stacked as high as my head. If they fell on me, I would have been toast.

Over the course of three months, I sold the entire inventory, along with everything else from other deals I had made for over $15,000. My office and garage that were perpetually filled to the brim with cards & memorabilia were now empty.

It felt like a chapter of my life was coming to an end. Never in the ten years of wheeling & dealing did I ever not have something to sell. There was ALWAYS something that would keep me busy, but this last deal wiped me out. It felt so final. Sitting at my computer in January of 2015 and writing up an article about it seemed like I was signing off from the dealer aspect of the hobby for the last time. I felt accomplished but somewhat empty. Happy, but sad.

I think the chaos that came along with all kinds of stuff to sell leaving so abruptly could be described as how you feel when you have a big party at your house, and everyone leaves. One moment there is mass commotion of laughing and overlapping conversations, but when you close the door after the last person leaves, all you hear are your dogs licking themselves. Over the next couple of years, I would continue to buy and sell cards, though not nearly in the volume that I used to.

You Really Made That?

Did You Know?

The picture used for Ken Griffey Jr.'s 1989 Upper Deck Rookie card was altered to show him as a member of the Mariners. He was actually wearing a hat from his minor league team, the San Bernardino Spirit.

With no new collections to purchase on the horizon, I had time to think about how I wanted to stay in the hobby, what I wanted to do and why. Did I just want to be a dealer who would take pictures and write about my purchasing exploits to share on my blog? It was great fun for me to do, but didn't seem like the only way I could get enjoyment from the hobby.

BECOMING A CUSTOM CARD CREATOR

I'm a big fan of online forums. I love them. I frequent Blowout, Freedom Cardboard, Collector's Universe, Net54, Beckett and the Sports Card Forum whenever I can. I'm most active on Blowout because that is where the most activity is. One night when I was browsing the website for any interesting tidbits about baseball cards, someone posted up a link having to do with 2013 Topps. It got me to thinking - Why hasn't Jose Canseco had any new mainstream licensed cards for several years?

It was almost as if Jose was blackballed from baseball cards once he wrote his tell-all book about being blackballed from baseball. A quick search on the Beckett website shows 254 results when you search for the phrase "2005 Canseco". When you search 2006, 16 show up not counting printing plates. 2007? 7. 2008 yields no licensed cards at all. In fact, you have to wait until 2014 for Jose to be featured on mass-produced, licensed cards again.

In the middle of this Canseco cardboard drought, I would often wonder what a Canseco card would look like from say, 2009 Topps or 2013 Topps. Then it hit me: Why not make them? Surely I could figure out the artwork - I had been creating graphics professionally for several years at this point.

Dreaming of what could be, I cracked open Photoshop and made my first custom card: a 2013 Topps Jose Canseco card as a member of the New York Yankees. I thought I would have fun with the online collecting community and printed it out on paper, then carefully cut it out with scissors (I can't cut a straight line with scissors to save my life!) and placed my handiwork in a top loader. I then took a picture of it with some real 2013 Topps cards that were on my desk, making sure not to catch the shine of the foil from them in the photo so that way they all looked the same. I posted a thread about it and asked people if they were aware of a short printed Canseco in 2013 Topps that wasn't on the checklist. I was excited to see what controversy I could stir up!

Almost immediately, people called my bluff so just like that, the jig was up before it started. Regardless, I had a lot of fun and was amazed at how close I could make a fun card that didn't exist using Photoshop, printer paper, and scissors, crooked edges notwithstanding. It made me wonder what else I could do if I really put my mind to it.

CANSECO COMES TO HOUSTON

I heard that Jose was coming to town, so I had an idea. What if I were to create some custom cards and have him sign those? This truly excited me - to create cards that didn't exist of Jose so that I could have my own personal custom 1/1s of him. I ended up making a few Allen & Ginter style mini cards of him that came out great. I didn't yet know how to create refractor or Superfractor cards, so I had Mark, a very talented and well-known custom card creator make some for me for the show. The results were very impressive and excited me even more to have Jose sign them. Holding various custom color refractor cards of Canseco from 2009, 2011 and 2013 Topps was awesome. They were incredibly beautiful, and no one else had them except for me!

While Mark did the refractors and Superfractors, I was up until 3 am the night before the signing, and woke up at 7:30 to finish up the Allen & Ginter style mini customs myself. To make sure everything went off without a hitch, I purchased a number of markers for testing purposes to see what would give me the nicest looking signature. I settled on blue sharpies for the refractors &

Superfractors and a thinner red sharpie for the mini cards. I drove to the card show where he was at and stood in line with my heart pounding in my chest just like it did when I was in line for his autograph the year prior. I was eager to show him what I had made.

When it was my turn, I was able to show him the work I had done. He studied them carefully and said *"Really? Wow, these are cool!"* When it came to the mini cards, he signed them and said: *"This is the smallest autograph I have ever done!"* I asked him to mark each of them as a 1/1, to which he obliged. A mere four months later, Topps released his first real Allen & Ginter card. They had him sign the /10 version in red and had him hand number them out of 10, so the customs I created to have him sign of 2011, 2012 and 2013 meshed in nicely with the real deal from 2014 and beyond. It was nice to not only have cards that I wished had been, but to know that he signed my minis first, before any others for the card companies. The best thing was that Canseco complimented me on them. It was such a great day!

RECOGNITION FROM PLAYERS AND CELEBRITIES

Jose isn't the only player I was able to get autographs of on my customs. Later on in the year, I was able to meet Tom Glavine, Craig Biggio, Frank Thomas, and Nolan Ryan. Talk about writing fodder! I was able to write up stories of my meetings with them, show off my work and receive all kinds of positive feedback. While the baseball players were great to meet, my favorite encounter was with Frank Thomas. He absolutely loved the work that I showed him.

Eventually, this grew into a TTM (through the mail) autograph obsession that wasn't just limited to baseball players, but to celebrities as well. Surprisingly enough, I received positive feedback through the mail from various stars and celebrities. Tony Danza wrote me saying that he liked and wanted a custom card I did of him - a Superfractor style card of him as a boxer. Nick Offerman, the actor who played Ron Swanson in Parks & Recreation also wrote to me. He didn't give any feedback on the card, but he did write me a note as a response to what I had written to him. At the end of my letter to him, I wrote this request:

"Would you please sign in the white area (of my custom mini)? It would be cool if you put 'bacon' as well, since I, too, am a fan of it."

When I received an envelope in the mail that said it was from Nick Offerman, I was excited to open it up and see if he did what I had requested. To my surprise, he wrote me a little note! Here is what it said:

"Tanner, I will try to please you, but the allotted space is to (expletive) small. - Nick Offerman"

You know it is going to be a good day when one of your favorite television personalities sends you a profanity-laced personalized message!

Shortly after my Canseco encounter, I just knew I had to learn how to create any type of custom I wanted, no matter the cost. Over the next few months, I spent a lot of time and money figuring out how to create my own cards that looked real. This included refractors, Superfractors, die-cut cards, relic cards, cut autographs, jumbos, booklets and more. I spent many late nights running to the store so I could get different types of cardstock, adhesives, and printable acetate to perfect my craft. I would stay up past 2 or 3 am designing, printing, cutting and gluing until I reached the desired effect. It was maddening and stressful, but well worth it.

I spent a lot of money buying supplies on eBay and arts and craft stores for testing purposes. I would often write detailed articles about my successes, failures and the end product, complete with pictures and anything else that was going on in life at the time. My articles would oftentimes be quite eclectic, but they seemed to connect with people. For more feedback, I decided to self-syndicate my articles by posting them on all of my favorite online forums. It is on these websites, after all, that I initially received the majority of my feedback.

I received so much praise, I felt like I found my own personal calling in the hobby by creating cards for my collection that didn't exist and writing about them. While I was not by any means the first or only custom card creator, (a quick eBay search shows over 10,000 custom cards are currently for sale) I quickly became one of the most well-known. Hearing how people thought my work was better than anything else they had ever seen, including what the card companies were releasing was truly thrilling. Some people would even send me high-end 1/1 cards and authenticated slabbed signatures worth hundreds or even thousands of dollars to create custom pieces for their collection.

There is something unnerving about ripping apart cards/memorabilia worth a small fortune to create something unique with no recognized "book" value. It is a strange feeling knowing there are high-end 1/1 checklisted cards that no longer exist because I was commissioned to make something that the owners wanted more. As long as they were okay with it, so was I. To make sure nobody would ever be deceived down the road into thinking my work was created by a card company, the backs of the cards would have a message stating it was a custom and would oftentimes show a picture of the card that was used.

ROLLIN' WITH NOLAN

Not everybody gets why anyone would want a custom card at all. One day, my family was at a book signing for our friend Kristin who just had her book published. We found out that the bookstore was going to have a Nolan Ryan signing a few weeks later. Nolan had come out with a cookbook, and they were selling them for $25 each, which would come with an autograph.

The cookbook had all kinds of wild concoctions in it. A taco-hot dog? Is that even legal? Whatever it was, I wasn't going for the cookbook. I was going for Nolan. I wanted to have him sign a custom. We purchased three tickets, and I ended up selling the autographed cookbooks to cover the cost of everything.

As I was standing in line waiting to meet Nolan, I was excited to be able to write to my audience about the experience. I was going to title it after an old Beckett article called "Rollin' with Nolan". If I recall correctly, it was an April Fool's story that talked about how Nolan Ryan went into a card shop looking to buy one of his own rookie cards. After finding out how high priced it was, he offered to trade the dealer some pitching lessons for it. The dealer in the fictional story declined.

The custom booklet wasn't the only card I created to have him sign. I also created a 1966 Topps style card of his, and two Topps football style orange refractors numbered 1/2 and 2/2. That way he could have one, and I could have one. Surely, we would chat it up, have a grand old time and he would thank me for the most beautiful card he had ever seen, letting me know it would stay on his nightstand for life. Sadly, that didn't happen.

I'm not sure if Nolan even looked up at me. He did thank me for the card, which was nice, and I would never say this encounter was rude or a discredit to the Ryan Express. I just think he was simply tired and ready for bed. He had already signed a number of items by the time it was our turn. Nevertheless, Nolan came through and signed my customs with some of the most beautiful signatures I had ever seen.

While it was an honor to have people send personal items from relatives or pets who have passed away to create a unique keepsake in card form for them, I was mainly doing it for my own collection, amusement, and pleasure. I was always thinking of ways to come up with something that no one had seen before - something that would make my collection more unique, and make people's jaws drop. From custom art pieces featuring authentic Babe Ruth and Mickey Mantle autographs to cards with cat fur embedded in them, I've done a little bit of everything. I still felt like I could take my creations to the next level by doing something extreme.

I DID WHAT WITH A GAME-USED BAT?

For the longest time, I wanted a Jose Canseco game-used bat, and was finally able to pick one up. With as cool as the game-used bat was, I never really collected whole game-used pieces. My mind immediately went to thinking about how many custom bat cards I could make. How cool would a bat knob card of Canseco be? How many slices of the knob could I get from the bat? Or what about a few bat barrel cards? The possibilities seemed endless. The question that plagued me for a long, long time was how to cut it up without damaging the prime pieces. I know nothing about cutting bats, and if I'm being honest, I don't know much about cutting any type of wood. If it were cake, then yeah – I'd be the guy to slice it up, but since it is wood, I figured I'd enlist some help.

I went on a several month long trek of finding the right person for the job. After researching forums, asking questions and learning about various types of equipment, I definitely knew I did not want to do it myself. I was able to find someone who was a woodworker and he was on a job site just down the road. He told me to meet him at his job with the bat, and he would update me with how it went.

After waiting for about 20 minutes, he finally met me at the base of a 40 billion story high rise building he was working on, and we talked for a few minutes. He took the bat and told me he would give me a call later on in the day to tell me how it went. That call never came, and he refused to return my messages. The man had stolen my bat! Thankfully, I only gave him a little league bat to test on first. I guess that was a very good $5 investment in knowing who not to trust my precious gamer with.

A while later, I found another fellow named Albert who lived in Louisiana. He seemed like a reputable person, and while he too had zero experience with cutting up a bat to my specifications, his work was top notch. He was there to answer all of the questions I had and was comfortable with the several page word document that I had prepared detailing all of my requirements. This document was a specifications list, complete with pictures telling him what types of pieces I wanted the bat to yield, with thickness, length, width, etc. I decided to trust him with my precious bat and shipped it off to Louisiana.

He showed me picture after picture with the progress of the de-constructed bat. From several bat knob slices to perfectly sliced bat barrel pieces and all kinds of other shapes & sizes I had requested. When Albert shipped them back to me, I was happy to see what looked like a lifetime worth of game-used bat material to work with for my personal collection.

A REAL GAME-USED BAT CARD

While I had already utilized a number of game-used bat pieces from my newly sliced & diced bat, one that I was really looking forward to making was a real game-used bat card. No, I'm not talking about a card with a piece of the bat in it. I'm talking about an actual piece of the bat being used as the card itself. I had Albert cut a few pieces to the size of a tobacco card, or an Allen & Ginter mini. It took a while for me to sand and perfect it, but I found a way to transfer my Photoshop handiwork directly on to the front and back of the wood piece. I left a spot for Jose to sign if I ever were to meet him again.

BASH BROTHERS BOOKLET THAT SHOULDN'T EXIST

The first custom booklet I had ever put together was of the Bash Brothers. What could be better, right? It always baffled me why no one had ever made one of these before. As it turns out, thanks to the book Canseco wrote, Mark McGwire allegedly will not sign anything having to do with Jose. As a fan of the Bash Brothers in general, that is a tough pill to swallow.

One night when I was in my office, I decided to try my hand at a custom booklet. I remember assuming it was going to turn out poorly, because I didn't know what I was doing, but I knew if I tried long and hard enough, I'd get it right. Because I didn't have any game-used material or autographs to use, I used an Oakland Athletics little league baseball hat I picked up from a garage sale for a quarter. It came out great, and I received a lot of great remarks from fellow collectors. Who would have thought hacking up a 25 cent little league hat would be so exciting to people? I loved it and was thrilled to know I wasn't alone!

A short time later, fellow collector Jason reached out to me saying he thought he could get Mark McGwire's autograph for me if I could get Jose Canseco's autograph for him. After thinking about it for a while, I wondered if I could make two separate pieces for Jose & Mark to sign individually, then turn the pieces into a booklet afterward. Surely Mark wouldn't have a problem signing a single card of himself without Jose!

I spent a good amount of time whipping up four cards total: two Canseco and two McGwire. I sent both McGwire cards to Jason so he could get them signed and I kept the Canseco cards so I could get them signed the next time I saw Jose. Right out of the gate, we knew that Canseco would be significantly easier to get than McGwire. As a matter of fact, several months went by without any possibility of a McGwire signing.

Just when I thought all hope was lost, Jason emailed me. He had finally tracked Mark down! Jason said that Mark paused for a bit before signing the card, which is understandable. As a standalone card, it did look a bit strange. While the card did have a small picture of his face on it, the majority of the card just showed McGwire's back. Why? Because that was only half of the picture. The other half was on Canseco's card doing the bash with him. After a pause, McGwire signed both! Jason then sent me the McGwire pieces, and I was able to create the first on-card Bash Brothers booklets ever. They turned out great!

Unfortunately, the story doesn't end there. Jason never did get his booklet, as someone had stolen his package from the mail. Thankfully, we were able to collaborate again and create a few different Bash Brother booklets.

JUMBO 12X CUT SIGNATURE BOOKLET

For every baseball fan, the best feeling you can have is when your team makes it to the World Series, and wins. For me, that point was in 1989 when the Powerhouse Oakland Athletics, took their cast of super stars & veterans to beat the Giants.

I remember being glued to the television and begging for my parents to put the game on the radio if we had to drive somewhere during game time. I also remember the earthquake – and feeling it, too.

I remember Dave Stewart being virtually un-hittable. I remember the swagger that Canseco and Henderson had – they oozed confidence. The infectious smile of Dave Henderson. The dominant and fearless look that Dennis Eckersley had each time he took the mound.

I also remember being heartbroken when one by one, my heroes were traded off or retired. The A's were no longer the same team I had rooted for. Nevertheless, the 1989 Oakland Athletics will always be my all-time favorite!

One of my favorite pieces in my collection is my game used 1989 World Series baseball signed by the entire team. While I love it, I wanted something that was in card form. The card companies will likely never make anything really cool that commemorates this team, so the gears in my head started turning.

I have already done a Bash Brothers booklet, so what should I do this time? Should I add Walt Weiss? All 3 were consecutive ROY award winners, and played in the '89 World Series. But, what about the man of steal, Rickey Henderson? Would it even make sense for those four to be together? Eckersley and Dave Stewart, too. What about Dave Henderson? Speaking of Dave, what about Dave Parker? I'd be a fool to forget Mike Moore & Terry Steinbach.

As you can see, I had a lot of things floating around in my head. I decided to start researching how to get autographs, and slowly but surely I was able to gather who I wanted. It was maddening to try to find autographs that would work though! Index card autographs were typically too large, and some players didn't even have autographs available online.

I would say among the most difficult to obtain workable autographs were Terry Steinbach and Mike Moore. Steinbach's signature is long, and Moore's signature is tall. As a custom card creator, you quickly learn that if you are building a custom cut signature card, the autographs need to be the right size.

Through eBay, friends of the players and mail-in donations directly to the players, I was able to secure all 12 autographs I wanted to use. My collection consisted of various signatures on blanks, in person autographs and certified pack pulled autographs. Some signatures were on sticker and some were on card, with all being obtained from different places. Clearly, I was going to be working with a very diverse group of autographs.

Based upon what was available, I knew that this wasn't going to be a project made of clean, perfectly signed white autographs, all in unison on a sterile design. This was going to be an explosion of colors and styles. I was perfectly fine with this, because that describes the 1989 Oakland Athletics to a tee! The next question was how do I get all 12 autographs to fit on one card?

Though I had never done it before, I opted to create a jumbo booklet that was nearly a foot long, so six signatures could fit on each side. It took several hours to create, but I was able to make something I was truly proud of that represented the starting players of my favorite team, the 1989 Oakland Athletics.

THE INVISIFRACTOR

Custom cards weren't the only things that I wrote about. One morning, I decided to have some fun, so I wrote up a press release about a card that I invented: The Invisifractor. A card rarer than the Superfractor! Here is what I wrote:

An unofficial Spokesman from the popular baseball card manufacturer has confirmed an extra surprise in the retail version of a new 2012 release. Something rarer than the Superfractor. The Invisifractor. A slickly designed card using cutting edge technology to give the appearance that it is invisible.

"You can literally see right through it," the unofficial spokesperson said in an exclusive interview.

"The best part about it is that when placed on top of a regular base or chrome card, the card actually *becomes* an Invisifractor. It is truly remarkable. It is so rare in fact, that there is not a serial number anywhere, making each Invisifractor rarer than a Superfractor. Yes, that means that it is a 0/0 card."

One has been pulled from a box at a well-known retail outlet, though, the lack of markings on the card make it difficult to substantiate the claim. When asked what he was going to do with it, the proud new owner mentioned that he is going to put it up on eBay.

"I'm going to make a killing off of this puppy! Imagine the value of a Superfractor Stephen Strasburg, combined with a

Superfractor Bryce Harper. I'm going to be riiiiiiich! When purchased off of eBay, the owner should IMMEDIATELY send it off for grading, as it should certainly receive a 10."

While some are not clear about if this is a hoax or not, others claim they see right through this shameless shenanigan to score some easy money to buy some more baseball cards.

For the fun of it, I posted it on eBay just to see what would happen. Lo and behold, people started bidding. I laughed pretty hard because the auction was literally for an empty top loader. To remove any doubt, I posted a joke video on YouTube explaining what it was and showing it – that it was literally just an empty top loader.

Still, people continued to bid. When this continued, I publicly stated that I would not hold the winner to paying whatever the end price was, just in case they didn't get the joke. If they did end up paying, I stated the money would go to charity.

At the end of the auction, the final price was $122.49, making it perhaps the most expensive empty top loader ever. My favorite thing about it all is that my term Invisifractor has been widely used in the hobby to describe a missing hit from a pack, empty mail day packages, and more.

MOUSTACHE FOR SALE

In 2015, I fulfilled a life-long dream and grew a handlebar moustache. I've always loved them, and my Grandpa Graham had one. Simply put, I don't think there is a cooler thing you can do with your facial hair! I've received tons of compliments and people have even asked me to pose with them for pictures.

Later in the year, a collector by the name of Kelly reached out to me, mentioning Rollie Fingers was going to be in town and asked if I wanted an autograph, to which I replied with an enthusiastic yes! I ended up making a dual card of myself &

Rollie, naming it "The 'Stache Brothers". Kelly showed Rollie the card, and he liked it! He put down a beautiful signature next to his picture, and when I received it, I signed my portion. I figured I would never have a real baseball card with a baseball legend, so this was the next best thing.

Shortly thereafter, people suggested that I create a card of myself with a hair from my moustache. Topps did it with a tiny piece of hair from Abraham Lincoln, so why not? Instead of the measly little speck of hair like the Abe card had, I went above and beyond. I equipped my card with what I called "The Alpha Hair". The longest strand of my moustache. Straightened out, it was nearly 2 inches of manly moustache hair. The former top dog of my upper lip. It didn't care if I was speaking or not – it draped down past my bottom lip like nobody's business. In addition to this, I embedded the tag from my camouflage baseball style cap. This is the hat I'd wear everywhere. The card came out very nice as a dual relic, and I topped it off with a red signature.

The plan was to put it up for auction on eBay, starting at 99 cents. Whatever money it would bring in would go to help fund my family's mission trip to Mexico that Holly and Atticus were going on that Summer. I posted this on multiple forums and thought it would be fun to run a contest. The contest was to post a guess of how much the moustache card would end for at auction. With countless entries, some of the higher guesses were $750-$1,000. Let's face it though, that's crazy. Heck, a tenth of that would be crazy. I'm not even a baseball player - let alone a superstar baseball player! Still, it was for a mission trip, so I gladly welcomed it going as high as it could.

The person who guessed the closest price of the ending value at auction would get a custom rip card, designed by yours truly. Within the rip card was a mini card telling them to go to www.TheMouschiCode.com - a website I set up with a number of trivia questions. When the winner got to the end, they would receive a prize. This may seem elaborate, crazy, and insane, but I have so much fun doing things like this that are out of the norm to entertain my fellow sports card collectors. This hobby should be about fun and enjoyment, so I do everything I can to make it that way. The auction ended at $416.98. There is more to the story, which is all documented on my website if you want to learn more at www.TanManBaseballFan.com.

CUSTOM CUTS

Since so many people were coming to me with custom card requests, I came up with an idea of creating a cost-effective kit for anyone to create custom cards on their own. The idea was simple: Give anyone the ability to quickly and easily create a custom cut signature or relic card on their own within five minutes, and have fun doing it. Within a week or two, my idea was launched and available for order. Over the past couple of years, I've enjoyed seeing countless people show me what they have made, from movie ticket relic cards to jumbo patch cards of their favorite little leaguer. My Custom Cuts kits are still for sale at www.CustomCutsOnline.com.

HOW DO YOU DO THAT?

For a while, I would get the same question multiple times a week. *"I want to make customs. Can you teach me?"* I completely understood why people would ask because not too long ago, I was in their shoes as well. I asked the custom card makers before me for help and found that no one was willing to share any techniques at all.

I was in awe of how beautiful their work was and wanted to make my own. I quickly found that I would have to learn everything myself. It wasn't until I spent countless hours and dollars figuring out how to create customs on my own that I realized why no one wanted to freely give out any information!

Teaching other people the techniques of creating customs was heavily frowned upon by many of the original custom card creators before me, and I didn't feel it was my place to do so, even though I had learned on my own. Out of respect for them, I kept my mouth shut but tried to be as polite and helpful as I could to those who would ask me, without crossing any boundaries that I didn't feel comfortable with.

Unfortunately, some people were not pleased with me for not sharing the techniques I learned, and some were even vocal about it as if I owed it to them. Nowadays, there are tutorials online that can be used, and I look forward to one day putting one together myself, as time permits.

CUSTOM CONTEST

Over the years, I received a lot of requests to create a special 1/1 custom for family members to commemorate a special occasion, or to have a keepsake of their playing days. Some would utilize an embedded hospital band and tape measure used on the day their child was born. Others had me create a cut signature card of a recently deceased family member using a canceled check.

From customs with embedded cat fur and claws to customs with guitar picks and chopsticks, I always enjoy putting together personal high-end customs the most, because of how excited the recipients are when they get them. Oftentimes, they tell me my creation is their favorite card in their collection!

Not everyone can afford a custom though, so in addition to inventing a cost-effective solution in Custom Cuts, I decided to run a contest, where I picked ten people who entered to have me create a special 1/1 custom for them for free. Throughout the month I ran the contest, I chose people based on their story and created something for them.

Putting together a card of a child in the hospital with their game-used little league patch and sending it to them is just one of many ways custom cards can brighten someone's day who is having a hard time in life. Though it was very time consuming throughout the month, the responses I received from the contest winners made it well worth the effort!

Chasing Canseco

Did You Know?

The 2004 Upper Deck Signature Stars Jose Canseco baseball card actually depicts his twin brother, Ozzie Canseco. Topps duplicated the error on Jose's 2017 Topps Archives baseball card.

Over the years, I've had dreams of meeting Canseco. Not just at a card show, but on a more personal level. One such dream placed me as a fan at the 1989 World Series. I was standing near the third base line, and a foul ball was hit in my direction. It rolled to my feet, and I picked up the game-used 1989 World Series baseball to keep for my collection. If I recall correctly, Jose was playing left field in my dream, and we exchanged a few words. Though the dream only lasted a few seconds, it felt real, and stuck with me.

A CRAZY IDEA

As I was returning from attending the Tri-Star baseball card show in 2014, I had an idea, and I just couldn't shake it. Could the countless Canseco customs I poured my heart and soul into over the past year all get signed at a *private* signing?

When I got home, I decided to reach out to his manager to see if a private signing was possible, and he promptly replied with pricing and terms. The price was much higher than I had hoped for, so I asked for a "budget" version to make it possible. We were able to agree on a price, so it looked like it was all going to work out! I just didn't know when.

He mentioned that Jose would be in the Houston area within the next month or two, but that wasn't going to work for me, as I wouldn't have everything ready for him to sign. Plus, I still had to get my head around the lunacy of having a private signing for me alone. Whenever you hear of someone doing a private signing, others will typically pay for autographs as well. If this was going to happen, I wanted it to be for me alone so that I could get all of my customs signed for my collection.

The next several months were full of uncertainty. Plan after plan fell through, and I began to lose hope that it would ever happen. When the signing started to sound hopeless, I made the decision to send the customs to a signing he was having up north. It would be a tragedy to make all these customs, and not have him sign them! It would have been much better to personally show him my art pieces, but I didn't want to run the risk of holding out for something that may never happen.

As a last ditch effort before shipping my customs to the signing he was having, I figured I'd check with his manager one last time to see if there was any chance of a private signing. He responded very quickly by saying *"Don't send the cards to the signing – wait until in person."* I was literally in the process of packing them up to ship out when I heard this. When I received his email, I put the packing supplies away and kept my handiwork on my desk. Could this signing really happen?

During Jose's home run tour in 2014, it looked like he was going to visit Texas again (albeit a long ways away from us). The plan was to meet up with him there. His manager called me (the first and only time I spoke to him on the phone, though there are countless emails between us) and told me the details of the event. He said Atticus and I could shag fly balls in the outfield during his home run tour. Yeah, I knew there were probably going to be tons of others doing the same thing, and I may not be able to say much to Jose, but that would be incredible. What a dream it would be to shag fly balls being hit by my childhood hero side by side with my son!

I got really hyped up for this, and as the date drew closer, I grew a little anxious, because I hadn't heard anything. About a week before we were about to leave, I emailed to ask for the details so we could wrap up our plans. He wrote and said the promoter canceled the event. I was really bummed out by this information. I had been dreaming of this for months! Just like that, I was a week away, and yet again – my dreams were dashed. I reached out to his manager again to see when Jose would be in the area. Over the next several months, several things fell through once again.

PLANNING A ROAD TRIP

Holly mentioned to me *"Why don't we drive to him?"* (She is a road-trip-a-holic). His manager said that would work, and after about a month, we figured out the day. The whole thing was nerve-wracking due to our plans failing each and every time in the past.

A week out, I nervously emailed to confirm, and his manager assured me that Saturday would still work. This was exciting news, but the problem is I didn't know specifically when or where we were going to be meeting him. I just knew that we were driving to Las Vegas to be there on Saturday. He said he would let me know the specifics later.

I knew writing down everything would be important because I would probably be so star-struck, it would be a challenge to remember my name, let alone what pen to use for what custom. I constructed an entire document to make sure I got everything right. I even planned on a number of bat pieces to get signed from the game-used bat I had cut up. Some of which, I stained black so that he could sign in silver and gold marker for variety.

I made a list of what inscriptions to write, the pen sizes to use, and more. I had every single little detail down on paper. I even built blank mock templates so that way he knew where specifically to sign on each item. This would prove to be very helpful so that I could make customs of them later. In addition to my custom pieces, I also brought along a small hoard of memorabilia such as jerseys, gloves, hats, cleats and more.

The time finally came for us to leave. As the start of our road trip began, I couldn't fathom that we were on our way to having Jose Canseco sign several things that I had created. To say it was unnerving that we were driving across America without a specific time or place is an understatement. I had a hard time swallowing the fact that I was driving countless hours without any definite plans. Yes, that's right – we had no idea where we were going or what time. But when this opportunity pops up, you have to shoot for the stars and go for it!

Still, there was a lot of doubt and concern. What if, when we get there, (after 20+ hours of driving) he cancels? What if I never hear from his manager again? What if Jose has to make a trip out of state for a more pressing obligation? More thoughts came to mind. What if Jose was in a bad mood and just signed everything then walked off? What if he signed with his shades on and earbuds in? What if he was just a cold jerk that would not be willing to do any inscriptions I had requested? What if the private signing takes place in public, and he spends the entire time talking and signing for others who came up to him? I had no reason to believe any of these things, but I always tend to end up painting the worst case scenario in my head.

After driving for 20+ hours, I had a lot of time to think about these things, not to mention the year leading up to this! As you can see, there were a billion things that could go wrong here. Would I be having a fire sale of my beloved Canseco collection if he was horribly rude to my family and me? What would happen then? How would that affect the rest of the trip? How would I feel about the incoming Canseco cards that would be waiting for me at home?

GETTING ON THE ROAD

Day one meant 13+ hours of driving to Albuquerque, and in the middle of this, we ended up getting caught in a massive hailstorm, the likes of which we had never before seen. As the hail came down and hit our car, it sounded like we were seconds away from having all of our windows shattered. It was incredibly scary, and we prayed for protection. Thankfully, we got through it safely. Holly thought a tornado was coming because the rain and hail were going sideways.

We made it to our hotel and I was still concerned as we were now nearly 900 miles away from home, and there was no word of where, when or how we were going to be meeting up with Jose.

I emailed his manager and said that I would be booking a Las Vegas hotel in the morning, and will send him the address so Jose can either meet us there or wherever he wanted. At this point, I really just wanted to hear something ... anything from him. We went to bed, and I woke up to an email from his manager.

"I will let you know where Jose wants to meet."

Talk about a HUGE sigh of relief! I was still on his radar. At least I had heard something, so it sounded like we were still on.

We got on the road and drove the last leg of the trip to Las Vegas which was 570 miles away. Small victories continued to be proclaimed each time we crossed state lines, and Atticus' illustrated map of the United States continued to be checked off with every passing different license plate. (We checked off all of them but Rhode Island!)

Before we left, Holly organized an event for some other moms and their kids to put together things called "blessing bags". These are bags filled with items to give out to homeless people on the side of the road. We were able to put them to good use on our trip.

After a few more hours of mundane driving (Holly had taken the wheel for a while) I received an email from Jose's manager:

"Jose wants you to come to his house at 12 for the signing. Here is the address..."

I just started laughing. Holly asked me what I was laughing about and I just read Jose Canseco's address out loud.

Confessions of a Baseball Card Addict

"NO! THAT'S NOT HIS ADDRESS IS IT????"

"YUP! WE ARE GOING TO CANSECO'S HOUSE TOMORROW!!!"

My favorite baseball player, the former best baseball player on the planet just invited my family over to his house! That one email changed this whole trip from a mission to get autographs, to a life experience that could far eclipse getting my customs signed. A true lottery winning feeling. I had spent this whole past year so focused on getting my customs signed and "finished", that I hadn't thought much about actually getting to hang out with him.

During the rest of the drive, all of my previous concerns changed. What if he just met us in his garage with his shades on and earbuds in? What if he didn't say a single word to us then barked at us to get off his lawn? Either way, going to his house, regardless of how cranky he may be or how rushed it might feel, was still beyond cool. Needless to say, I don't remember much of the drive after that.

We made it to our hotel, and went to sleep. I woke up the next morning, and stared at the over-sized clock showing 5:00 in big red numbers. Seven hours until I was at his house! Surely my stomach would be in a thousand knots, and I'll not be able to speak English, but in seven hours, ready or not, we'll be there. About 10:30, an hour and a half before the signing, I got a text from the manager.

"Can u make it at 11 instead of 12?"

This really got me all knotted up. Was this an ultimatum? If I couldn't make it there by 11, would it not happen? We hadn't even checked out yet, and were a half hour away. I texted him saying I thought I could make it by 11:30, and he wrote back:

"Okay, I'll tell him you are on your way and will be there at 11:30. Please hurry!"

That one text turned my morning from one of fairly peaceful preparation to total chaos. We hastily packed up everything, checked out, got directions and started driving. Was the "get there ASAP!!!" text foreshadowing how hurried/rushed/cranky Jose may be?

After only one wrong turn, we finally got there. We drove up to Jose's beautiful house. The garage door was closed, so that meant I was going to be ringing Jose Canseco's doorbell. Unreal!

GOING TO MY HERO'S HOUSE

We got out of the car, and the weather was perfect, with sunny skies. I brought my huge tub of items to be signed, and after I rang the doorbell, I heard dogs barking inside. Jose Canseco's dogs. There was a massive elephant tusk art piece on the porch that made me wonder how he could trust people not stealing such an impressive piece just sitting on his porch. I looked back at Holly in bewilderment with an "I just rang Jose Canseco's doorbell!" look on my face while she was grinning from ear to ear. I felt like I had won the lottery, just by being able to ring his doorbell.

After a while, the door was opened by a young woman. It was Leila, Jose's girlfriend at the time. I had often thought about how this scenario would play out. I wondered how she, as a model, would act. A lot of times, you might think of models as being rude, cold, self-absorbed, etc. I knew nothing about her, or even if she would be there, yet here she was opening the door to let us into their home. It was beyond surreal to see her in person. This very woman could be found in many pictures all across the web on my childhood hero's arm.

As we walked inside, there he was. The incredible Cuban hulk – the man I invited to my birthday party many years ago and didn't come. The guy who was the best player in baseball when I was growing up had just motioned for us to come over to his kitchen table. He had just finished laughing with Leila telling her that after he mowed the lawn, a bird pooped on him. I resisted my urge to ask him to buy the shirt that the bird had pooped on to make a custom out of it. That would have been weird to do...right?

He cleared off some space on the table, and I lugged my huge tote onto it. I started by giving him a deck of cards I made for him.

"I know you like poker, so I made these for you...here." I gave them to him, and as he shuffled through them, he said:

"Are you serious? Whoa! These are cool! Leila! Come here and take a look at these!"

Leila came over and looked through them, too. "Wow, these are really cool! They came out very nice!" Jose told me he has friends come over every week or two to play poker, and they would be using the deck I made for him. Later on, I told him to look at the back of the playing cards. I made a custom back for each of them with my face and name in the design of a standard type of playing card, that way it was subtle and not too in your face.

"Ha! Tanner!"

I was thrilled that he said my name and would be using them with his friends to play poker. I'm very glad I made these for him because he was incredibly happy.

As I got out some things to sign, the whole situation was very nerve-wracking. Thanks to the text I got earlier, I knew he was in a big hurry, and I did not want to put my favorite baseball player in a position where he had to throw us out.

Every piece I brought for him to sign had a note stating what type of pen to use and what to say. The first piece I had him sign was a Triple Threads style of card that was to be signed in silver. I gave him the wrong pen to use, and the signature looked horrible. I asked if I could use his sink to see if I could quickly clear off the bad signature from my poor choice in pens. He said no problem and went to put on a baseball game for us to watch while we were doing the signing.

All that time spent making the card, and all the pressure to get done fast, and here I was – at Jose's sink, carefully, yet feverishly rinsing off the card. It ended up coming off, and he was able to put a better signature on it. One down and 164 more to go!

After this, things went smoothly. Leila brought Holly & Atticus outside to the backyard so they could see their tortoises. I have to say I was pleasantly surprised by Leila. Not that I had any reason to think otherwise, but I always seem to have a "worst case scenario" view of situations like this. She was so sweet to us all, offered us drinks and chatted with Holly the whole time. They hit it off very well, and even fed the tortoises, which by the way are awesome!

NOT JUST A SIGNING

While I was excited about having Jose sign all of my custom pieces, that was only half of the story. In the past several years, card companies have begun inserting pieces from jerseys that have been marked as "player-worn". These are jerseys that were worn by a player, but not necessarily in a baseball game. Jerseys from workout sessions, photo shoots, and more have been cut up to be used in cards. I figured if the card companies could do it, then so could I.

This is the whole reason I brought along various jerseys, hats, gloves, cleats and more. They were for Jose to wear, so I could have a virtually unlimited supply of player-worn material to make custom cards with for my collection.

It took a lot of work tracking them all down, but I was able to secure a proper jersey and hat for every single team he was with. I even had some relevant All-Star & World Series patches sewn onto the jerseys. It would be fun to see my favorite baseball player wearing jerseys for each team he was with for one last time, and perhaps for the first time since he played with them.

I first pulled out the fielding gloves. I brought three of them – one being a lefty because I had no idea if his finger was in good enough shape to wear due to the gun accident. The good news was that his finger looked great, so he put on a glove, and started banging the middle of it with his fist.

"Man, this is a really good glove!"

He kept saying how much he liked it, and then the unthinkable happened.

"I might have to trade you one of my game-used gloves that I use in baseball games nowadays for this."

I almost jumped out of my skin when he said that! What baseball fan wouldn't want to make a trade like this with their favorite player?

I told him I would love to trade, but if he wanted it, he could just have it. I quickly followed that up by saying I would love to trade. He mentioned it might be too small, so I prepared myself for the deal not to happen. Right at that moment, he hopped up and disappeared into his room. He came back with his glove and traded me, saying he knew he could make it work!

To make things even better, he asked for a specific marker I had and laid down a perfect inscription in silver ink. It looked beautiful against the game-used black leather. He said he used it to pitch with and play third base as well. I promised him this was one glove I would not be cutting up. He said, *"Yeah, do not cut this one up!"* Are you kidding, Jose? I'm taking this to my grave! (I didn't say that, but that is what I was thinking.)

After this, Jose started to educate us all on how he breaks in gloves. He started by placing his new glove from me in the microwave and said he would probably work on the glove by pounding it, rolling it and stretching it for about an hour to get it ready for his next game. As great as it was that he traded me gloves, it was also awesome to hear that he planned on using my glove to play with in future games!

Afterward, he put on the cleats I brought, but they did not fit well at all. While sitting in his chair, he started doing a funny tap dance with them partially on. We all got a kick out of it! He told me after his playing career, his feet had grown bigger. I called Atticus over, who was 12 at the time and showed Jose his feet.

"Wow, you are going to be tall!" Jose said. My son answered, "That or I'm going to be a hobbit!"

Jose was right. At 16 years old, Atticus is now probably taller than him!

He tried on all the hats while Holly and Leila were talking, so she wasn't taking any pictures at that time, but when it was time for the jerseys to be put on, Jose said we should go in the backyard for this so that we could take good pictures. He read my mind! Holly got several shots of him wearing each one. He was great and posed for each picture. I couldn't believe at 50 years old, how great of shape he was in. He looked like he could still play at the major league level.

The A's jersey was the last one he put on, and I was able to pose with him for a picture while wearing my A's jersey. After we were done, I was concerned about taking too much of their time, but he kept talking to us. He told us about all the neat animals that come into their backyard.

When we went back inside, I had him sign each and every letter on all of the jerseys he tried on. I have always loved the nameplate letter cards, but they seem to typically be manufactured letters and not from actual jerseys that were worn. I loved when Topps came out with "Own the Name" cards, but think they would be so much cooler if they were signed. Having him sign each letter was the best of both worlds, for each team he played on. This was one of the most important parts for me of the entire trip.

The agreement of 165 autographs I had purchased in this deal was coming to a close. Though Jose wasn't keeping track of how many things he had signed, I didn't want to overstep the agreement I made with his manager, nor did I want to overstay my welcome. I told him that I did not pay for two of the jerseys to be signed on each of the letters, which meant 14 additional autographs. I said if he had the time to sign them, I would be happy to pay more.

He could have easily just said he would gladly sign more, and have me pay extra, but he didn't. He refused my money and signed the extras for free.

"Please … don't worry about that! I'll sign them all for you, no problem. Heck, you made a really awesome playing card deck for me."

Some of the cards I had him sign caused him to ask questions. Like my request to have him inscribe H.R. #500 5/9/03 – I told him this was for a card I called "What If" and said that the date coincides with my birthday. He then understood and signed it while telling me if he had one more year in baseball, he would have gotten to 500. I wholeheartedly agree with him! The man was 37 years old the last time he played baseball and had so much athletic ability left in him.

Another card he questioned was one that I made of him as a Simpsons character. Jose played a part in one of the most well-known Simpsons episodes ever made, "Homer at the Bat". In this episode, Jose Canseco, Don Mattingly, Darryl Strawberry and tons of other players made guest appearances. The script called for Jose and Mrs. Krabappel to have a torrid love affair. Jose's wife Esther allegedly did not like this one bit and insisted it was pulled. This put the writers of the Simpsons in a scramble to come up with something else last minute. They instead had Jose go into a woman's house that was on fire to save various objects from the fire.

As I gave him the card to sign, I asked him to personalize it to Mrs. Krabappel.

"Mrs. Krabappel...that is a strange name." I said *"That is the name of the teach..."* and he interrupted me by finishing my sentence *"OH OH OH yeah ... the teacher on the Simpsons, ok!"* Step aside, Madonna! It looks like Mrs. Krabappel had his affections back then.

Having him sign all of the cards from my custom collection got quite messy. He was great, but I had all of my cards outside of their holders so they could dry. They were all over his counters and kitchen table. Mismatched one touch holders of various sizes were all over the place and would have been virtually impossible for me to put back together within a reasonable amount of time. I did the best I could by stacking everything up and carefully placing them in the tub I brought.

During the signing, he mentioned something about showing us some home runs of his that he guaranteed were never seen by us before. Monster home runs that were hit further than his famous 1989 ALCS SkyDome home run. This was something I was very much so looking forward to!

It made me wonder, why hadn't he kicked us out already? The signing was done, and here he was still talking to us. He went to get a disc his father had made him that included interviews and home runs he had hit. It didn't work because he only had a blue ray player, so I suggested that I get the laptop from our car outside for it to play on and he said okay.

We popped in the disc and watched the whole thing together while he was narrating. Sure enough, some of the home runs he showed us were more incredible than any I had ever seen.

One part of the DVD that we watched was part of an interview with Jose wearing the game-used batting practice jersey I picked up a few months prior. The jersey had pills in the pocket, to which I still have, of course! Holly said to me *"Hey, isn't that the jersey you have?"* And Jose said, *"Yup, that is the same one!"*

Before we started watching, Leila had just made cupcakes for us. Jose and Leila offered us some when she took them out. When Jose Canseco offers you cupcakes, you do NOT say no. They were delicious! After watching the home runs, he talked to us about home run length, bat speed, size and more. When he was finished, he had us come upstairs.

He led us into his poker room where two beautiful poker tables were. One of which had some incredible artwork done of him. He told me again how much he loved the playing cards I made him and put them on the table for Holly to take a picture. He fanned them out and said, *"Here is a better shot for you."*

We had a seat at his card table, and he kept talking about the glove, then we ended up playing cards! He asked me what I wanted to play, and being someone who doesn't know much at all about cards, I was drawing a blank. Go Fish? Memory? Old Maid? None of those sounded like good options, so I suggested Black Jack. We ended up playing several hands. Holly asked for another picture of us, and I was reminded about one pose I completely forgot about: The bash! How could I leave without a picture of us doing the bash? Apparently, I put my arm in the wrong place, so Jose re-positioned it a few times. It was a rookie mistake on my behalf, not having ever bashed with Canseco before.

When we were done, we went downstairs for us to pack everything up and go. He insisted we take several of the cupcakes with us on our trip, which we agreed to do. I asked him to autograph one but was kidding. Thankfully, he knew that because if he had signed one, I wouldn't have been able to bring myself to eat it. Well, okay. I would have absolutely eaten it - they were really good! The cupcakes he sent with us lasted a total of 30 minutes or so between Atticus and me.

As we walked out the door, I thanked him for having us over, and we walked to our car to leave. We had one problem, though. Through all of the amazing picture taking Holly did, she left our keys and her phone on the poker table upstairs. Yikes! I rang the doorbell again, and Jose answered with Leila this time.

"I'm so sorry. Holly left our keys and her phone upstairs."

"Oh, no problem, come on in!"

I scurried up the stairs to retrieve them while they were still in the kitchen. I shook both of their hands and thanked them once again for everything, then walked out the door.

I am still in shock about how everything went. Everything I brought was signed and all memorabilia pieces were worn. We traded gloves, ate cupcakes they made for us, fed their animals, played cards and watched his home runs while he narrated for us. I don't know how it could have been any better. It was an absolute dream come true! Scratch that. It was better than anything I could have dreamed.

Just being there to hear him talk about how the bird pooped on him was fun. Later on, we got on the subject about what would happen if a robber broke into his house, and how he may throw an apple as hard as he could at the guy. Yes, the guy who hit 40 home runs and stole 40 bases in a single season was telling us about how he would throw an apple at a robber!

The entire signing and such probably would have taken 30 minutes, but he entertained us for a few hours. For me, the verdict is in – both he and Leila are very hospitable, warm people who went above and beyond what my expectations were. Initially, getting my customs signed and having him wear everything was something I had considered to be the pinnacle of my collecting "career". Something that could never be topped. But in the end, the intangible experience of hanging out with him for the afternoon at his house far eclipsed that.

As we drove off, I might as well have been floating. My car now had tons of player-worn and autographed game-used material that I could use to create tons of custom cards for my collection. It truly felt like I hit the lottery. In many ways, I felt like this was the ending to the book I always wanted to write. Somehow though, it just didn't seem like an appropriate ending to my collecting story, and I wasn't sure why. My story just felt incomplete. What else could top this?

WRITING ABOUT THE EXPERIENCE

When my time with Jose happened, I was excited to share my experience with the online card collecting community. The night we got back to our hotel, I cracked open my laptop when Holly and Atticus were asleep. I started writing about all that had transpired while it was fresh on my mind. By the time we made it back home, my entire story about the experience was nearly ready to share.

After putting the finishing touches on it, I posted my story on my website and all the major card collecting forums. Tens of thousands of people read about my experience and wrote congratulatory notes. It was suggested that I reach out to Beckett Magazine to see if they could do anything with it. Could it be possible that my story could be in my favorite magazine of all time?

GETTING TO BECKETT ONLINE

After a while, I reached out to Beckett and was told they would be interested in my story. They said they would run the article as a special online piece. I was thrilled! Little did I know that this was just the tip of the iceberg.

Shortly after all this had happened, I received a tweet from Chris Olds to check the Beckett website. Not knowing what to expect, I quickly typed in the website address, and to my surprise, a large picture of Jose and me doing the bash was front and center on the website! I could not believe my eyes. Clicking the image of us took you to a huge article, complete with pictures of the experience.

BEING PUBLISHED IN BECKETT MAGAZINE

Shortly thereafter, I received word that my story would soon grace the pages of the actual print magazine itself! It has always been a dream of mine since I was a child to be featured in Beckett magazine. I assumed this would be a black and white quarter page feature, but it turned out to be quite the opposite.

When the August 2015 issue of Beckett Magazine hit shelves all across America, someone who had a subscription reached out to me to show pictures of my feature. My story wasn't just a tiny quarter page black and white blurb. It was six full-color pages showing off pictures of Jose and me hanging out, along with several of the custom pieces I had made. It was the largest article in the entire magazine. Not only that, but they even put us on the cover of the magazine itself! Pictures from all over the United States were sent to me by other collectors. It was crazy to see a picture of Jose and me doing the bash on the cover of a national magazine, sitting next to magazines with celebrities and models.

When I finally received my copy of the magazine, it was such an incredible feeling. When I finished reading the article, I had a "what if?" feeling about Canseco's most notable card: His Rated Rookie. What if there was movement on it in the price guide? If you are a child of the '80s or '90s, you know what I'm talking about. You would live and die by the arrows next to cards in the Beckett price guide.

102

With this being the first current Beckett I held in my hands for quite some time, I just had to take a peek. What I found was truly thrilling to see. His Rated Rookie card did, in fact, have an up arrow next to it! In fact, out of the thousands of cards listed from 1948 to the early 1990s, it was one of only three cards in the entire price guide that had shown a bump up in price. I asked someone who worked at Beckett if my experience could have caused this, and he said it was entirely possible. I was thrilled to hear that I may have caused a bump in price for a card that was once one of the most coveted baseball cards in the world.

MY BASEBALL CARD APPEARANCE

Another one of my dreams was to be on a baseball card. Shortly after all of this happened, Beckett announced on their website that they would be producing a sports card set of 15 cards exclusively available at The National Sports Card Convention (NSCC) at the end of the month. These serial numbered cards would depict trading card sized Beckett Monthly covers featuring various back issues. Various booths at the National would have these cards available. If you were one of the first 200 to go from booth to booth to collect all 15 cards and present them at the Beckett booth with proper documentation, you would receive a special autographed card produced by Beckett.

Someone sent me a visual checklist, and to my surprise, one of the cards in the 15 card set was my cover with Canseco and me doing the bash! This meant the world to me. Since Canseco was on the same card, it also meant that my card would likely be in the collections of other Canseco collectors as well.

I count all of this as the wildest blessing that could have ever happened to me in this hobby. Did hanging out with Jose at his house really happen? I'd pinch myself and look at the custom card he inscribed and signed for me:

"Tanner this is awesome work! Your friend Jose Canseco"

We have communicated a few times since I was at his house, starting with him messaging me later on in the year after we hung out just to check in and see how my family and I were doing. Since then, he has requested some custom cards of mine which I happily made and sent him.

It all still seems like a fairytale to me, but as I quickly learned, my journey in this hobby was far from over.

If These Cards Could Talk

Did You Know?
Topps used to give gifts to players in exchange for using their images on baseball cards. One year, Willie Mays complained about the toaster he received from Topps, saying it was burning his toast, and asked if it could be repaired.

About a year and a half before going to his house, I sold my childhood collection of Canseco cards. I came to this decision because my collection lacked direction. I was amazed at how few "special" cards I actually had - especially since I spent years stockpiling all the Canseco cards from the millions of cards I had gone through. I had 50 of the same Topps base card, but not a single refractor. 20 1994 Pinnacle, but not a single Artist Proof. Stadium Club? You bet! First Day Issue? Nope. My collection lacked deeply in the parallel department. The intention was to one day create a checklist, see what all I had, determine what I needed, and "do it right".

Even though I had gone through more cards than 99% of people in the hobby, I still came up short of having anything truly unique or special. The items that were most valuable were due to the memories attached to them. The 1989 Fleer card that he signed on the cellophane wrapping I put over the card to protect it in its journey through the mail. The autographed baseball my grandparents gave me. The shirt I wore as a child to support Jose when he was traded to the Rangers. These were the things that were most valuable to me - perhaps only after realizing nothing else had much monetary value.

SELLING MY CHILDHOOD

After thinking about it, I realized the intangible memories attached to these pieces were far more valuable to me than the items themselves. In October of 2013, I listed my collection for sale on eBay for $999.33 or best offer. The shipping? $40.40, naturally. I took pictures of my binder, the box with doubles, 8x10s, plastic gas station cups, magazines and everything in between.

A few short weeks later, someone made an offer and ended up buying it all. I took the afternoon saying goodbye to my precious collection, packed it all up and shipped it out. For the first time in my life since I was nine years old, I found myself living in a home with less than five Jose Canseco baseball cards.

COMING BACK TO COLLECTING CANSECO

It didn't take longer than a couple of months for me to come back to collect his cards again. This time though, I wanted to do it right. After a few key purchases using the funds from my old Canseco collection sale, I amassed quite a nice selection of die-cuts, refractors, inserts, and others that I had never seen before in the millions of cards I had shuffled through over the years. This made it clear to me that assembling a world-class collection would not come from just throwing money at more cards; it would take a great deal of time and effort – being intentional and deliberate about collecting the right cards.

I found out quickly that there were collectors of his who were willing to pay a small fortune for his rarer cards. Around the time I started back up collecting again, I saw an unimpressive looking 1/1 card with a small bat chip sell for over $450. This floored me! How could someone pay that for such an unimpressive card? I wanted absolutely no part of collecting 1/1 cards if that's what was going to happen. I planned to focus on cards I enjoyed looking at, instead of highly valuable cards of him. That mindset did not last very long, though.

Over the next several months, the hobby I loved since I was a child became more exciting to me than ever. I went from being a casual collector of parallels to purchasing a few collections from former heavy Canseco collectors, one of them being former Canseco Supercollector Paul. He had already sold a number of key cards, but I was able to pick up a large portion of what he had. What came along with these cards were countless interesting storylines. To me, collecting is so much more than just pieces of cardboard with pictures of baseball players on them.

Collecting is also about the thrill of the hunt, the camaraderie between collectors and the stories behind the cards. Where did they come from? How were they acquired? A good example of this is a Topps buyback Canseco card I picked up. From the outside looking in, it is a $5 card at best. To me, it is worth so much more because of the story behind it. Gary Carter Supercollector Anthony actually pulled it from a pack with Lauren Shehadi on camera while they were on the MLB Network, and he sent it to me for free.

Within these collections I picked up, were cards that had not seen the market for several years. These collections contained cards that were fought hard for. Some were picked up from intense trading sessions, and others were unearthed from tirelessly sifting through countless boxes at local card shows from back in the 90s. Still, others were picked up from chasing a lead online about certain mythical cards existing when no one else had known anything about them previously. I have a ton of appreciation for these cards and the history of how they made their way into my collection.

Somewhere along the line, a switch was flipped, and I was no longer casually looking for cards I thought were cool; I was intensely searching for any and all Canseco cards I didn't yet have. This happened when I realized that there were significantly more cards on my "have" list than on my "want" list. It was no longer about just getting the cool looking cards that I enjoyed looking at. A card could be as ugly as sin, and if I didn't have it, I'd want it.

I still remember a couple of cards that I lost out on while I was en-route to Canseco's house. The fact that it "hurt" missing out on a few pieces of cardboard with Jose's picture on them while I was going to meet up with him shows you how much baseball cards mean to me.

Perhaps all of this was the perfect storm for me to transition from a casual collector to a Supercollector. While I have many stories to tell about buying, selling and trading, here are a few of my favorites.

MY FIRST 1/1

The catalyst for becoming a Supercollector might have started with my first 1/1 purchase. As a Supercollector, 1/1 cards are typically the most sought after. The best of the best. There can only be one 1/1, and there can only be one owner of said 1/1. With stiff competition, I knew that getting even one 1/1 was going to be a hard thing to accomplish. A few short months after I came back from Jose's house, I landed my first. A 2015 Topps Tek Black Rainbow. I even remember where I was - at a stop light on my way to church to pick up Atticus from Youth Group. The seller spelled his name wrong in the auction title - "Conseco" and I was the first on the scene.

With a few clicks, I was the proud owner of a 1/1 Jose Conseco ... errr... Canseco. I was elated to have finally beaten all of the other big Canseco collectors. This was a huge deal because it seemed as though all of the "good stuff" was being hoarded by a group of five or so people, with no one else ever even having a chance. I had often wondered if there was going to be room for me to get any special 1/1 cards at all. The ability to purchase this card gave me hope.

A TALE OF TWO WHITE WHALES

One day, a big-time baseball card collector named Bob reached out to me after reading an article I had just written.

"I enjoyed viewing your Canseco cards. One card I didn't see was the '88 Topps Cloth Experimental A's Leaders. Do you have that one?"

The question he posed was extremely exciting to me. Could he possibly have the card he was asking me about? I

Confessions of a Baseball Card Addict

quickly wrote back and said I did not, asking if he had one available. After a while, he responded with something that knocked me back.

"The card is yours for free if you want it. Just send me your address. I'd love for it to be part of such an amazing collection."

I was beyond flabbergasted that this man would give me such an amazing card for free! After a while, he showed me another card, stating "Unfortunately I only have one of these." He sent a picture of a 1989 Leaf Blue Chips Canseco card. Though the 1988 Topps Cloth was the oldest prototype card on my want list, I'd have to say I wanted this one even more. I wrote him immediately, and he confirmed my suspicions: It was not for sale. I wrote him and asked if there was anything I could do to change his mind. He said no price would be possible to get him to part with it.

A few days later, while Holly & Atticus were away from home, I received a knock on the door. I opened up, and it was the mail lady. She handed me a box, and I wasn't sure why, because I wasn't expecting a package. I opened it up, and its contents stunned the living daylights out of me. It was the 1989 Leaf Blue Chips card! Thankfully, my family wasn't around to hear me squeal like a little girl. Bob sent me not one, but two amazing cards for my collection out of the goodness of his heart.

Bob's generosity is something that our hobby desperately needs more of. I constantly hear about people in this hobby who try to scam others, so to remember Bob and his kindness is truly refreshing. I should mention also that Bob has an insanely amazing baseball card collection himself. If you ask me, he is more than deserving of every last card he has, and a whole lot more!

THE BAT KNOB THAT (ALMOST) GOT AWAY

2016 was a monumental year for Jose Canseco baseball card collectors, because of the latest Topps release of Tier One. It featured the first and only (at the time) autographed bat knob 1/1 card of Jose. Armed with a search engine and enough time, you can oftentimes find the exact game-used bat that was purchased by the card companies to cut up. If you are lucky, you can even find a picture of the player using said bat in a game to photo match it.

I was on high alert for this card and was unsure of how much it would sell for, as nothing like this had ever shown up on eBay before because it was the first of its kind. The only thing I could compare it to was Canseco's first 1/1 button card that sold at auction in the $1,200 range a year or so prior, which I was able to acquire later.

A few days after the product had released, I was waking up from a nap and checked my email. Well-known wax aficionado Kurt had just sold me a couple of Canseco cards and was writing me to acknowledge my email to him stating I received them safe and sound. Or so I thought. His email was a little different than I had expected:

"Did you get the 2016 Tier One Canseco bat knob auto? I saw it just sold."

WHAT?!!! I would have likely never known about the knob, had I not emailed Kurt thanking him for the cards he sold to me. Feverishly, I checked the sold listings and couldn't find it. After a while, I was able to locate it. It quickly became clear why my searches were unable to see anything. The seller had listed it under the name of Jose Gansego. The font that Topps used made it look like it was spelled that way. EBay did not show it as having been sold, though. It just showed that the listing had ended, so there was hope! I reached out to the seller to ask if he had it available. I was excited to hear that he did still have it.

We ended up agreeing on a price, and a deal was made. Or so I thought.

He told me there was a catch. He had already agreed to a deal with someone else, though the card was still in his possession. Because of this, he was willing to back out of the previous deal. When asked what the name of the buyer was, he spoke the same name as one of my biggest competitors. On more than one occasion, this competitor of mine reached out to multiple people I did deals with to try to buy cards out from under me, even though I had already paid. Could this be sweet payback? No, I couldn't do it. Even though I wanted the card badly, revenge did not sit well with me at all. Saddened, I declined to do such a thing, but as a last resort, I asked the last name of the buyer just to make sure.

Much to my delight, it ended up being a completely different person than I originally thought! Not that it would have changed anything, because I still wouldn't have purchased it out from under someone else, but perhaps the buyer would be willing to do a deal with me since he wasn't a Canseco Supercollector. I knew if it were my competitor, he would lock it up in his collection no matter what I offered, forever.

I reached out to the buyer and offered to send him money on the spot, if he allowed me to purchase the card from the seller instead. He agreed, and the card made it into my collection. It felt like a roller coaster ride to get it, and the cost of admission was high. Both the buyer and seller were paid very well, but it was well worth it for the clear conscience.

CRUSADE EXECUTIVE SAMPLE

One day, I was perusing Worth Point to see if any cards stuck out to me so I could do some Internet sleuthing and perhaps figure out who the owners were. I found a couple of cards, and as it turned out, I knew who the seller was. I reached out to him, and he said he sold the cards years ago. After doing a little bit of begging, he looked through his sales records, and was able to find out the buyer's contact information, even though the purchases were made years ago.

The cards I found were green and purple parallels of 1998 Donruss Crusade. I already had a green and purple, but these were extremely special. They were Executive Samples, which meant that only 1 or 2 likely existed of each.

I reached out to the buyer, and he ended up responding fairly quickly. We talked on the phone for a while and hit it off. He already knew who I was, but I had never heard of him before. That isn't uncommon for someone who may have a card or two I don't have, but this was much, much different.

After talking to him, it sounded as though he may not only have just a couple cards I didn't yet have but about 50. Simply put, this never happens. I do not ever run into someone who has more than a couple I don't yet have, so 50 was unreal - especially from someone whom I've never heard of before.

To make sure there was no miscommunication, he sent me a high-quality video showing his entire collection, and sure enough, there were a legitimate 50 cards I did not yet have.

Among these cards were low numbered parallels that had not seen eBay since before I had entered the collecting arena. I was truly dumbfounded. After looking at everything, I made an offer of $5,000 for his entire collection. I figured I would be able to make my money back on some of the duplicate items. The conversation sounded very optimistic as if it was about to happen. He told me he would think about it and get back to me. I had high hopes but didn't hear back for a while. After a couple of weeks, I decided to check in, and he told me he probably could not do it. The reason? His wife.

Never in all of the years that I have been in baseball cards, had I ever heard that the wife was the reason *not* to sell. He clearly has a keeper! He mentioned that while she wasn't completely against it, she definitely wasn't for it. I bumped up my offer by $1,000, and he said he would take it to his wife. With as promising as his first response sounded, this one sounded even better.

A few more weeks passed by, and I checked in again. Sure enough, it was the same story. His wife didn't want him selling for what I offered. I was taken aback because I knew I was offering good money, but sometimes it just doesn't work out. Drastic times, however, call for drastic measures.

I went through his video again to make a list of all the cards I didn't yet have. I determined that I could expect to pay $6,000 total if I were the winning bidder for all 50 cards at auction. I had gone from $5,000 for his entire collection, to $6,000 for a mere 50 cards. If you are not a Supercollector, this will give you a glimpse into how our minds work. We see a bunch of cards we like and make a good offer. We wait and wait and wait, only to be turned down. Eventually, all we can think about are the cards we missed out on, and offer unreasonable prices. Rejection breeds obsession.

Now mind you, $6,000 for those cards wasn't completely unreasonable, as I truly felt that is what they would have gone for on the open market, but I don't care who you are. That is a lot of money. That was how much my beloved 1989 IROC Camaro cost me when I was a teenager, and here I was making an offer of the same price for 50 baseball cards.

This offer definitely piqued his interest. Enough to pull each and every card, and take a picture to make sure that we were talking about the same cards. Once more, he said he would talk it over with his wife, and once more I had to wait a little while. But that was okay, because if this wasn't a slam dunk, then I didn't know what would be.

He came back to me apologizing for the wait and made a counteroffer. Since so much time had passed, I figured that would be the case. If I truly felt these cards were worth $6,000, then I certainly would be willing to pay a bit more as a premium, just because there were so many cards I needed in one spot. I was ready to play ball!

At least, I thought I was. The owner came back at me with a price of $18,000. Triple the value of what I would expect these to go for on the open market. I was truly in disbelief and didn't know what to say. But, when you have this type of opportunity, you absolutely have to go for it as a Supercollector, so I sent the total $18,000 that evening.

Okay, I confess - I'm pulling your chain. I did not pay the $18,000. What I did was rack my brain trying to figure out how to get a deal done with someone who is trying to sell 50 cards at above 1/1 prices, when very few were even close to being that rare.

When I realized the deal wouldn't work out, I politely declined, and we parted ways. Over the next several months, I would check in just to see where his head was at, but he wouldn't budge. When all is said and done, I could probably say he was a mirror image of me in many ways. I have zero qualms with how he handled things and was glad to have met a truly nice fellow collector. It stung that we weren't able to get a deal done, but what can I say? You can't win them all. A year and a half later, I ended up doing a deal with him for the one card I was most interested in that caught my eye enough to seek him out in the first place: The 1998 Crusade Green Executive Sample.

PULLING AN ALL-NIGHTER WITH COMC

Check Out My Cards, (COMC) is a well-known website that thousands of collectors flock to in order to fill holes in their collections, find deals and flip for profit. While eBay gets much more traffic, COMC is definitely a website that you should keep an eye on.

Every now and then, you will see certain sellers list an insane amount of amazing cards. COMC doesn't give its users the luxury of being able to message each other, though that isn't necessarily a bad thing. As a seller, sometimes you just want to be left alone and list your cards for sale. If a buyer wants a card, they can either buy it or make an offer, and a seller can either accept, counter, or decline. Simple as that.

One seller that many collectors would love to get in contact with has an unreal inventory of obscure, back door and prototype cards. One day, a collector reached out to me as a heads up to tell me a lot of super rare '90s cards were coming up for sale on COMC. I was on high alert because of this and started visiting the website more frequently, so I didn't miss anything big.

One night after dinner, I remember haphazardly checking COMC on my phone. Nothing new was listed other than some base cards. I moved over to the sold section, and my heart stopped. A 1997 Pinnacle Totally Certified Platinum Gold was sitting there.

How could I have missed this card? Who got it? How much did it go for? All kinds of questions rushed into my head, and I didn't know what to do. I had advertised all over the Internet in hopes of landing this very card, stating that I would pay a $50 finder's fee just to be able to purchase it. There are very few cards that match its beauty.

As I kept looking at the sold listings, I noticed a distinct difference between it and a few other cards. Others had sales data, and this didn't. Is it possible that this wasn't sold, but rather just showing as sold because it was stuck in some sort of queue, waiting to be listed? I had no idea if it was a fool's errand or not, but I wasn't going to leave COMC unattended anytime soon.

Fellow cardboard enthusiast and Will Clark Supercollector Ryan noticed this as well for a few rare Will Clark cards. We kept in touch over the next day to report to each other if any sold cards moved to the for sale section. I stayed up late that night on my computer, doing nothing but wearing out the refresh key on my keyboard. I dug further into the sold listings and saw many other amazing cards that I knew for a fact hadn't seen the active side of COMC. I felt that at any moment, these cards could be listed, and for all I knew, there were 50 other rabid collectors out there obsessively hitting refresh at the same time I was.

While I did get some sleep, it wasn't much. When I get fixated on something, I have a hard time catching any z's. I woke up very early and scurried over to the computer to begin a long day of playing finger meets f5. My wife walked in while I was doing this, and was puzzled.

"Uhm...Babe? What are you doing?"

"I'm Pinnacle hunting. Totally Certified, baby!"

"You have a problem, sir. Seek help!"

Clearly, she didn't understand what was at stake. Later on in the day, after hours of absolutely no movement, some Will Clark cards popped up. I notified Ryan, who was able to grab the cards he wanted on his phone while he was at the store. I was happy for him, but what about me? What about the cards I had been so obsessively searching for?

Just like that, some new Canseco cards were listed. Some Leaf Executive Prototypes, a 1/1 with its serial number missing, and others. Finally, the Totally Certified surfaced, also with no serial number. It is the only one I have seen without the numbering, ever. I clicked purchase as quickly as I could and became the proud owner of the card I had been dreaming of. Well, day-dreaming that is. When all was said and done, I was able to purchase every single card that showed up that day.

DRAINING A PRODUCT IN TWO HOURS

By the time 2017 rolled around, I was firmly planted as the main Jose Canseco collector for nearly a year. It seemed as though if anyone saw a rare Canseco, they would reach out to me more often than not. I would get multiple messages a day pointing me to all the best cards. It helped tremendously because I knew that I was positioned better than anyone else to get the first choice of whatever I wanted.

When 2017 Tier One came out, I was excited because while having the only knob/auto card (from 2016) was great, having the only two knob/autos would be better. Plus, they were also due to release a beautiful autographed barrel card. The pictures of the cards that were showing up on eBay from other players were absolutely gorgeous, so I was on high alert.

The thing with 1/1 cards is you never know if they will be opened from a box in a day or five years. Even then, you are not guaranteed to see the 1/1, as it might be pulled and stuffed in a box in someone's private collection, never to be seen again. For the Canseco collector, the autographed bat knob and autographed bat barrel cards are highly sought after, so everyone would be gunning for them. Within a few days of the 2017 Topps Tier One release, I was notified of both cards and was able to do a deal for them with two separate sellers, all within less than two hours of each other.

SACRIFICING A WOOD CARD AND SUPERFRACTOR

As a Supercollector, you rarely, if ever will sacrifice a 1/1, and certainly not a high end 1/1. In 2015, collector RandyB on the Blowout forums reached out to me to let me know that a 2015 Museum Wood Jose Canseco card was pulled in a break. The Beckett checklist noted this as a /3 card, but after looking at the video, it was clear that this wasn't a /3 - it was a 1/1. This card was absolutely gorgeous. Constructed completely out of a thick piece of wood, the "card" (if you can call it that!) was wrapped in a wood frame and topped off with a silver ink signature. The card was breathtaking.

After a series of emails to and from the owner, I was able to acquire the card and counted it as one of my favorites. This card especially made waves in the Canseco collecting community because everyone wanted it. Who could blame them? For months, fellow Canseco Supercollector AJ kept begging me to do a deal with him for it by offering multiple 1/1s, other rare cards, and cash. I had no intention of selling though. This baby was staying in my collection forever.

A few months down the road on a Wednesday night, AJ and I were on the phone in the middle of one of our epic trade battles - not including the wood card, of course! These trades would typically be drawn out for days at a time. I told him I had to go, but he insisted we stay on the phone until the deal was completed. I probably told him I had to get off the phone two or three times, but it was clear that there was no getting off the phone with him unless I hung up on him, which I wasn't about to do.

Just then, in the middle of him telling me it was important we stay on the phone to finish our deal, Canseco's first autographed Superfractor ever popped up on eBay! I was able to purchase the noteworthy card while he was mid-sentence. Had he not stayed on the phone, it would have been very possible I would not have been able to get it. I decided to keep my mouth shut after the purchase, and stayed on the phone to wrap up the deal with him as well. A few days later, he called me.

"Did you buy the Superfractor?"

"Yup!"

"Ugh. It was during our phone call, wasn't it?"

"Yup!"

A few months later, we started talking about the wood card and the Superfractor - how he would love both cards in his collection, and how it was getting tiresome for him to continue chasing 1/1s. After talking it through, I decided to sell him both cards for $3,333.33. There was, however, a contingency: He would have to give up buying 1/1s released from 2017 and beyond. I figured this would help me tremendously going forward. In the end, it worked out nicely because not only would I have less competition on 1/1s going forward; AJ was able to secure the card he lost out on when we were on the phone. The biggest downside for me was that I no longer had my precious wood card. I set my hopes on being able to get the next one Topps would release, though there was no guarantee that would ever happen.

A few months down the road, Topps started showing mock-ups of 2017 Museum. The digitally rendered pictures did not make it look like the wood cards were going to be made completely out of wood. They looked like they were merely going to have wood frames. This was hugely disappointing, but I held out hope, thinking that perhaps Topps didn't show a full wood version because they didn't yet have real pictures of them.

A week or so before the release, the checklist I had been anxiously waiting for was posted. I quickly checked, and sure enough, Jose was going to have a wood card! Whether or not it was going to be a suitable replacement for the full wood card remained to be seen. When the set was finally released, I checked eBay to find any 2017 Topps Museum wood cards that were listed. I was excited to see the wood cards were in fact 100% wood!

It didn't take long for Jose's card to make an appearance on eBay. One morning while I was at my computer working, I was alerted to it being listed. A huge rush broke my mid-morning lull, and without even paying attention to the card itself, I clicked buy it now for significantly less than what I sold the other wood card for. I spent no time whatsoever to inspect the card, read the description or anything. After I secured the card, I sat there catching my breath for a while. What did I just buy? Was this latest purchase the single thing that would make selling my first wood card okay? *Don't just sit there. Look at the card, Tanner!*

I went to my purchases section and stared at it for a while. Much to my delight, the card wasn't just beautiful; it was perfect. Everything about the card was significantly better than the one I had just given up. The wood was a darker finish, the picture featured Jose in a solid green jersey and was a close-up shot. The card was accented in gold holographic foil, and the card itself was signed in gold ink. Absolute perfection! This was, to me, a great ending to the story of the wood cards for Canseco.

THANKSGIVING IN LEGOLAND

Near the end of 2017, my family and I decided to spend Thanksgiving in Florida. The plan was to go to the beach and Legoland, with Medieval Times being our destination for Thanksgiving dinner. It was such a fun trip! The problem? Leaf announced they were going to release their new product during this time: 2017 Leaf Q.

Within this set were three different types of Jose Canseco cards, each with the biggest game-used patches in recent memory and several parallels for each card. As a player collector, I was extremely excited about the 2017 Leaf Q release. I was even more so excited given the fact that I already knew what they looked like.

Before their official release date, Leaf showed some examples via Twitter, and they looked absolutely gorgeous. The one card I was most excited about in particular was the 2017 Leaf Q Flashback 2015 1/1. In spite of it being an unlicensed card, it was perfect in every way. Discovering what this card looked like also ended a several months long mystery for me. I had picked up three printing plates from 2015 Leaf of a card that had never been released, seen or even mentioned before. As it turned out, the printing plates I had were of the Flashback card I was so excited about.

This card featured just the right amount of gold holographic foil to accentuate the best parts of the card, a perfect signature, and a jumbo patch. Not just any jumbo patch, though. The largest green & gold elephant A's logo patch I had ever seen on a Canseco card. It was almost as if Leaf had found a way around the logo licensing issue by featuring a massive patch that showed the A's logo right in the middle. They never printed the logo; they just let the patch do the talking, and boy did it ever. Scratch that - the logo didn't talk. It sang.

Needless to say, I was on high alert during the trip, knowing the card could be listed on eBay at any time. It could be while I was driving, getting gas, on a roller coaster or cheering for the knights that were putting on a show for us during Thanksgiving dinner. That specific card constantly popped up in my head while driving for several hours on our road trip. I'm not sure if I ever put that much brain power into another 1/1 before.

When I was in the passenger seat of the trip, I would occasionally hop on my phone to peek in on some Leaf group breaks and chat with other collectors to see if anyone saw the beautiful 1/1 surface. Because the live video feed wouldn't work on my phone, I had to log into my computer remotely by using my phone and watch the breaks as if I were sitting in my office. It made me feel like a hacker doing all of this from the passenger seat of our car, in the middle of nowhere.

While it was fun to play computer hacker for a while, this card brought a lot of anxiety for me during our trip. Not just because it was a card I wanted, or because it was a 1/1. I had tons of cards I loved already and more 1/1s of Canseco than anyone else on the planet. My anxiety was because it was THIS card. A card I had been dreaming about. For the Supercollector, the best card is not a specific card in your collection; it is the one you don't have yet that you seek to add to your collection. I feel it is important not to let feelings of entitlement take over because you aren't due anything. You simply cannot have it all, nor should you try. With all that said, I knew that if I missed out on it, I would not be happy.

A few days into our vacation while we were walking around in Legoland, my phone buzzed to notify me that a card was listed. I checked, and sure enough – there it was – on eBay! With a hefty price of $1,500, I couldn't just click the buy it now button.

Instead, I made an offer for $1,000 and camped out on another page to see other offers roll in. Anxiety crept in because it was such a special card. I knew it was highly possible one of my competitors could swoop in and hit the buy it now button. If that happened, the card would certainly not be let go for anything, so it could be considered good as gone forever.

Minutes later, I discovered someone else matched my offer, so instead of letting it go to chance, I hit the buy it now button myself. Thankfully, I had a coupon code to help on the price, and I became the owner of quite possibly the most beautiful Jose Canseco patch card ever made. I never thought I could love an unlicensed card as much as this. During this same trip, I was able to secure all three 1/1 Canseco cards from the 2017 Leaf Q set. The other two were gorgeous as well, but as with almost all other Canseco cards that have been made, they don't hold a candle to the 2017 Leaf Q Flashback 2015 1/1.

1998 PINNACLE CERTIFIED PROTOTYPE

When AJ and I first met online, he showed me some of the most amazing pieces of cardboard in his collection I had ever seen. One of which was the 1998 Pinnacle Certified Red Prototype. The card was beautiful, and sadly I'd never be able to own it. AJ had the only copy that had ever surfaced, and 99% of the collecting community had not seen another one of these for any player. This is because only a few were created before Pinnacle called it quits.

1/1s are special. They are manufactured to be special. There is something to be said, however, about prototypes like the 1998 Pinnacle Certified. They scratch an itch that 1/1s simply cannot get to, as they were not manufactured to be rare. Being the owner of pieces like this make you feel like you have something that you shouldn't. It is cards like these that haunt collectors for years. They are true unicorns and do not exist ... until they do. To me, the 1998 Pinnacle Certified Red Prototype did not exist outside of AJ's collection. Until three years after he showed me, that is.

It was a Friday evening, and I was about to head out of the office for the weekend, but decided to check eBay one more time. What was in front of my eyes made my heart stop. It was the beautiful Pinnacle Red prototype! Starting out as a 99 cent auction, my heart raced, and I made plans to make it mine, no matter the cost. If there was one card worth going all in for, it was this one. Normally, I wouldn't talk to other collectors about a card I was going for, but knowing that AJ already had this, I reached out to share my excitement.

"AJ, did you see the card on eBay? I'm so excited! I'm about to join the club!"

"Tanner, I don't have that card. This isn't the red. It is the *mirror* red."

My heart sank, as I knew this was going to be quite a costly acquisition if I was going to win the card. I wanted to get my hands on my first 1998 Pinnacle prototype - a version of it that had never been seen before, and AJ wanted to get his hands on it to match the one he already had. Since we did a deal previously where he had to stay away from new 1/1 cards, this was a lot more appealing to him. This was definitely going to be an uphill battle, but I was up for it. I checked the listing constantly to see where the bidding was at, and it didn't move much initially. Sunday afternoon, the worst thing possible happened to this card. It disappeared from eBay.

Extremely frustrated, I reached out to the seller who was unresponsive. The card was on my mind quite a bit that evening as I was driving to pick up Atticus from youth group. I kept thinking to myself *"How can I find a way to reach the seller if he isn't responding to me through eBay?"* I knew the seller was in the Dallas area, and though he too was in Texas, it was about four hours away from me. I tried to think of anyone I knew in his area that had to do with cards.

After thinking about it for a while, I remembered a guy who came down to the Houston area to purchase a few hundred thousand cards from me a couple of years prior. He mentioned he was from the Dallas area, so I figured I'd give him a call. After finally remembering his name, I was able to search my phone for his number and called him. I asked if he remembered me and he did. Dallas is a huge place, and to ask if he knew the person who listed the card would be a one in a million shot, but it was my only shot, so I had to try.

Have you ever met someone from another state and asked them if they knew your friend from the same state by their first name? I've done that before, and spoke the words without even thinking about how absurd it sounded. Something like *"You are from Ohio? Hey! I know someone from Ohio! Do you know someone by the name of Matt?"* I never once thought about how many thousands of people named Matt that may live in Ohio. Well, this time it worked!

I asked if he knew the seller, and miraculously, he did. What are the odds of that? He gave me his contact information, and I was able to have a conversation with the seller. It did not go well though. My worst nightmare was confirmed: He sold the card offline. There was no going back; the card was as good as gone.

The guy I knew from Dallas reached back out to me a day or two later and checked in with me, asking what I was looking for. I told him it was a Canseco card.

"What card?" he asked.

I told him it was nothing he would have ever seen before. A 1998 Pinnacle Certified Mirror Red prototype.

"I wish you would have asked me to begin with, Tanner. I think I have it. Give me a week, and I will get back with you to see if I do or not."

My excitement meter didn't move off of zero, because I was certain he was talking about the common 1997 version. This often happens to me. People will look at my want list and excitedly proclaim they have something I need. It almost always ends up being a common base card or another common parallel. I did not tell him this, of course. If there is one thing I've learned, it's that you leave no stone unturned. Plus, to get to this point seemed almost like a miracle. I had to continue down this path as far as it would take me. I told him I'd love to see a picture when he could send it.

A few days came and went, along with a few "what if?" daydreams about the card. Later on in the week, he gave me a call.

"Check your texts. I just sent you a picture."

He had it! Not only that, but he also had the base, mirror blue, and mirror gold - as well as the red that I had always loved so much that AJ had. Within an hour, we did a deal for the entire set of cards. Not only was I beyond excited that I was getting the entire run, I was also unspeakably shocked that the one person I reached out to had a card I was targeting. A card that, to the general collecting public, didn't exist. Had a deal not been done offline with someone else for the original card, I would have never seen the others. It truly seemed like divine intervention for this all to work out the way it did.

I still cannot believe how it all worked out, but my collecting journey is riddled with all kinds of stories like this. Yes, collecting is fun, but eventually, the cards just end up in a box. The experiences and stories themselves can sometimes be even more exciting. Every card has a price tag, but the memories made because of them are priceless.

How to Become a Supercollector

I'm going to be up front with you. Setting your sights on becoming a Supercollector should probably not be an aspiration in your life. There are far too many other important things to focus on. Supercollecting takes up a lot of money, time and brainpower. Did I mention money? Competing with other fellow collectors on rare cards can be very taxing on your psyche, and wallet! You may find yourself spending crazy money on numerous cards you don't even care about just because you don't yet have them.

ANATOMY OF A SUPERCOLLECTOR

Before I go any further, I thought I'd give it a shot to describe what a Supercollector looks like. Generally speaking, a Supercollector is simply someone who obsessively collects a certain niche (be it a player, team, etc.) with laser focus, and goes way beyond casual collecting. Supercollectors typically share many of these characteristics:

- There is an extremely clear and apparent intentionality about their collection.
- Their most vivid dreams are about landing a rare item.
- Their collection is heads and tails better than most in their collecting niche.
- Their spouse despises the object of their desire. (Mainly because the Supercollector typically goes overboard!)
- They have significantly more cards in their collection than cards on their want list, including the incredibly difficult to obtain pieces.
- They are considered by the vast majority of the collecting community to be a Supercollector.
- Their favorite memories in life have to do with capturing a super rare card.
- They may have a pet or child named after their favorite player.

- Vacations are planned around new card releases.
- When anyone asks a Supercollector what's new in life, their first thought is to respond by sharing what new cards they recently picked up.
- They have a room that looks like a shrine dedicated to the object of their affection.
- Non-collectors may typically think that Supercollectors genuinely have a problem. (That may not be far from the truth!)

To other collectors, a Supercollector's name is what may first come to mind when they think of the player they collect. For example, when I hear anything about Andre Dawson, I don't just think of his stellar career; I think about Dustin and his amazing Dawson collection, boasting over 150,000 cards of the Hawk alone. Whenever I hear anything about Mark Teixeira, I don't just think about how great of a player he was; I think of Robert and his jaw-dropping collection of over 1,000 1/1 cards of Tex. Being synonymous with a specific collecting niche is the dream of any Supercollector.

DECIDING WHAT TO COLLECT

When you set out to focus on collecting a player, team or other niche, you may not be sure which direction you would like to take or what parameters to set. One of the questions I heard the most was "What made you want to collect Canseco?" Many may remember him for the ball bouncing off of his head for a home run, his tell-all book and more recently, his eccentric tweets. I remember him as my childhood hero, the 40/40 man and the former best player on the planet.

Canseco was larger than life and he transcended the game. In his prime, if you didn't know anything about baseball, you still knew about him. The man even had a 900 number that his fans could call to hear a recording of him.

Throughout the years, I've picked up some amazing items of the best players in baseball history, but I never had the desire to keep anything. From a Mickey Mantle autographed baseball to a 2009 Bowman Chrome Mike Trout Blue Refractor autograph, I had no real emotional attachment to anything. Everyone would drool over pieces I had but they never excited me enough to keep.

Conversely, I was never so attached to Canseco the man that I wanted to collect everything with his face on it. I didn't go after magazines, posters, figurines, plates or other similar items. It was at the intersection of baseball cards and Jose Canseco that I found a deep love for Supercollecting. My intense passion simply wouldn't have existed without both! Regardless of the direction you take, be prepared to be called crazy.

When you set out to mark the path of your own collecting journey, you have to find what you are passionate about. Find out what excites you, and not just what interests others. Remember, there is no right or wrong answer in collecting. What you like may not interest others in the least, and that is okay. Collecting for the approval of others will leave you unsatisfied. When you set a path that excites you and stick to a budget for the hobby, you can enjoy collecting without any guilt.

I wholeheartedly endorse being a casual collector. There is more than enough cardboard to go around for those who casually collect. For the Supercollector, there isn't. You don't just want some cards; you want all of them. Nevertheless, I want to document my story, so in spite of my warnings, (do as I say, not as I did!) here is my story on how I came to be known not only as the #1 Canseco Supercollector, but also the poster child for Supercollecting baseball cards. (That's what many others have said, at least. I'd never be so bold to give myself that title!)

HOW I DID IT

There is a vibrant and active collecting community online. As a Supercollector, I had a choice to make. Be passive and merely pick up cards that showed up on eBay, or be proactive and make my name synonymous with collecting Canseco. To stay in front of the collecting community's eyes, I would frequently publish articles talking about hobby history and post prank stories. I would also display my latest pickups, write about my latest inventory acquisitions, post card collecting memes/gifs and feature my custom work.

My activities were an outpour of the passion I have for the hobby. I love cards, the collecting community and (almost) everything in between. As a byproduct of my efforts, I became known as the go to guy when someone had a rare Canseco card for sale. This wasn't all I did, though. I proactively used a number of methods to get the best Canseco cards into my collection. Here are some tools I used that helped me, and can hopefully help you, too.

TOOL #1: CRUSHING IT ON EBAY

Though I did get numerous private offers on a daily basis, many cards would still show up on eBay. Oftentimes I'd reach out to the seller, and they would tell me they already knew who I was. This was tremendously helpful, as people seemed to want to deal with me before they dealt with anyone else. Positioning yourself like this must be organic. There are several platforms that collectors frequent on the Internet to discuss cards, so saturating all of them in a friendly and helpful manner is very beneficial. I realize not everyone has the time or patience for that, but this is what I learned:

Be first on the scene

Tip #1 for eBay is to be the first one on the scene. This means obsessively checking listings. At any given time of day, I would have a browser tab open with eBay open to a Canseco search results page. This way, I could always quickly hit the eBay tab, press f5 and see if anything new popped up in a matter of seconds. I would do this countless times throughout the day.

Check misspellings

As I learned with purchasing my first 1/1, some people would spell Canseco's name Conseco. As I learned with the autographed bat knob card, they could also possibly spell it Gansego. With my eBay tab open at all times, I would not search "Jose Canseco". I would instead use a litany of combined misspellings and formulate it in such a way as this: (canseco, conseco, gansego) -jessica. The parenthesis would allow for me to pull up any listing that matched any of those words, and the -jessica notation would remove anything listed that had to do with his ex-wife.

Reach out to sellers

If a seller had something rare for sale (regardless if I wanted it or not), I would reach out to them to ask if they had anything else. You never know what else is hiding in people's closets. I've made several terrific deals with people doing this.

Do NOT ruin other people's deals

It is always a good idea to keep an eye out on the sold listings. It isn't necessarily a bad idea to see if you missed anything from time to time. You could even reach out to the sellers and see if they have anything else for sale as well. This has worked wonders for me in the past. I do not suggest trying to work a deal on a card that you missed out on by offering the seller more money than they agreed to sell to someone else for. That is simply bad form and will ruin your name in the hobby. Steer far clear from ruining any deals someone else may have already made.

Always be courteous

The longer time went on being the first on the scene, the more I realized my competition was paying closer attention to listings as well, and were also checking eBay significantly more than before. No matter who the seller was, I would always be polite and positive. I'll admit, this isn't really a "tactic" but rather human decency. My philosophy is always to be kind to others, no matter what. You never know what someone else is going through at the time of your interaction with them, or how your words will affect them.

When competing with other offers, being courteous could be the difference between missing out on a noteworthy card and landing something you want. I would always reach out and let the seller know who I was in an upbeat manner. If the seller had a higher offer from someone else or was planning on selling to someone else, I would always thank them for their time.

You never know how your kindness can affect people, and in situations like this, I was often awarded the ability to purchase the card, simply because the seller liked our interaction more in spite of someone else offering them a higher price! Even if things didn't work out for that particular card, I would sometimes hear back from the same seller when they had something else I may have been interested in, simply because they didn't like how the buyer of their other item treated them.

Don't bad-mouth your competition

In striking up conversations with many sellers, I was able to form several relationships with them. Because of this, they would tell me what my lies or deceit my competition would say about me. It was always the same few guys, and the amount of time and energy they spent bad-mouthing me behind my back was almost laughable. They were sick and tired of losing out all the time. The good news is that it almost always backfired on them, and I was seen as the more pleasant person to do business with, where they appeared very bitter and ugly. The lesson is this: Do not bad-mouth your competition. Just stay in your lane, and be pleasant.

Use the eBay app

Actually, don't. You don't need to be on your phone any longer than you already are. If, however, for some twisted reason, you want to become entrenched in the game of Supercollecting, the app is necessary. I would always have the app loaded up with the search results for new Canseco items (including the misspellings), so all I'd have to do is refresh the app and see if anything I was interested in was just listed. The app removes any concern of losing out on a card just because you aren't on your computer.

TOOL #2: ONLINE FORUMS

I first became active on the forums when I started collecting as an adult. My favorite and most frequented forums are as follows:

Blowout Forum

Freedom Cardboard

Beckett Message Boards

Collectors Universe

Sports Card Forum

Net54

Just like eBay, I would routinely search for Canseco's name on the forums to see what was available and eventually would search my screen name "Mouschi" just in case someone would post a scan and call out my name, without actually typing the name Canseco.

Branding and message

Every forum I was on would depict a caricature of myself as well as a familiar signature stating I was always looking to buy rare Canseco cards. My message was clear and constant, and my branding was consistent across all forums. I didn't just want people to know I collected Canseco, though. I wanted them to care enough to take the time to tell me about any rare Canseco cards they would find. That is a tough leap to make for many if you aren't offering anything of value, to begin with.

What helped me tremendously was that I would spend a lot of time taking my stories and articles I wrote for my blog and self-syndicating them across all of the forums by manually posting them everywhere. This was by far the best and quickest way for me to become recognized. All told, my articles and stories have generated hundreds of thousands of views, and many would tell me the only reason they logged onto the forums was to see if I had written anything new.

I didn't just want exposure though; I wanted to provide value and entertainment to those who were reading. Any articles or stories I would write would be to educate or entertain, but with a positive spin. They would never be used to tear anyone down. I think that is why so many people connected with what I was publishing. In spite of me posting a consistently positive message, not everyone would return the favor.

Dealing with the trolls

If you are on the forums for any amount of time, it is no secret that you will encounter a troll. A troll is someone who will come online to hurl inflammatory messages at an innocent bystander with the intent to cause them emotional harm. You will see this all over the forums and social media. Many will call these people "keyboard warriors" because they would likely only dare say negative things because they can hide behind an anonymous username.

Do not be misled into thinking that trolls are justified if they say they are okay with "speaking their mind" in person just as they are online. That just means they are consistently ugly people. The travesty for the troll is that with each nasty thing they post, they are publicly displaying what is truly inside of them - things that the vast majority of people go to great lengths to hide, out of sheer embarrassment.

With these unfortunate people, they "speak their mind" in the name of being courageous enough to speak the truth. The truth of the matter is that they aren't courageous at all. They are simply trading human decency for a few pats on the back for being clever or funny. If it blows up in their face or they receive any pushback, they will typically cry foul and complain that someone doesn't want them stating their opinion. In actuality, it isn't necessarily their opinion that is offensive; it is that they attempted to be hurtful in their delivery.

Now that we have defined what a troll is and what their motives are, it is much easier to take the next course of action: nothing. Try to ignore them. If someone says something to try and get a rise out of you, I know it is easiest just to lash back out, but remember this quote:

"Never argue with an idiot. They will just drag you down to their level and beat you with experience!"

It is typically a complete waste of time and energy engaging them, and there is no reason to give them even a millimeter of your precious brain space. If you must address something, then do it tactfully. Remember that your response is not for them, because they aren't worth your time. You are writing for the potentially thousands of others who are reading.

In writing something ugly, a troll has already publicly declared that they are a classless loser, not worthy of your time. By responding to them kindly, you are positioning yourself as just the opposite, and people will respect you for it. It may not get more eyeballs on your posts, but that is where you have to make a choice: Do you want to have a questionable name known by many, or a good name known by some? For me, I want to have a good name.

TOOL #3: SOCIAL MEDIA

I'll be the first to admit; I was late to the party when it came to social media. This was quite possibly my greatest tool to use for getting cards I did not yet have.

Instagram

I used this one the least by far, so I will not have a whole lot to say about this, but now and then, I would search Instagram for Canseco's name just to see what would pop up. From time to time, I would get lucky and find cards I did not yet have. Unfortunately, I had very little luck getting responses, but Instagram was certainly not a complete waste of time. Checking hashtags of not just your player's last name, but also of his full name and even the latest product he is in can potentially yield results. Admittedly, I probably would have had more success with Instagram, had I invested more time into it.

Twitter

I was really late to the Twitter game, but in a short amount of time, I amassed over 1,900 followers. This is not a lot compared to many out there, and I am not too terribly active on it, but whenever I post an article or story, I make sure a link goes on Twitter. The same goes for any YouTube video I post as well.

My most successful posts on Twitter were not my articles or videos, though. They were the funny memes I'd post with my website address on them. I would post graphics showing that Donald Trump and Barack Obama were encouraging others to contact me if someone had a rare Canseco card. Another was an animated gif of Jose Canseco swinging the bat using a series of baseball cards, in the style of a flip book. If there was a card I desperately wanted, I would create a "wanted" graphic with a

138

reward stating that I would pay anyone for information leading to the capture of the card pictured.

Successes and failures would be publicized as well. Basically, if there was anything I could do to keep myself in front of everyone's eyes in an entertaining manner, I would do it. And it worked! On many of my memes and gifs I would post, they would be retweeted several times, which meant more eyeballs on my main message: If you have a rare Canseco card, come to me before going anywhere else!

Facebook

I have been a Facebook user for years, mainly using it to post funny things and keep in touch with friends & family. It wasn't until the past couple of years that I learned of quite possibly the most active segment of the hobby community on the Internet: Facebook groups. There are countless closed groups out there with thousands of active members who collect baseball cards. These groups have proven themselves to be one of the most effective tools for growing my collection.

I quickly found that collectors and pseudo-dealers alike would go to Facebook and post their biggest hits to show off to the online community. I remember on a few occasions where I would post something telling people to show the first baseball card related picture that was on their phone. Within an hour, several hundred people posted responses! That goes to show you that a very large number of collectors are active in these groups.

I would also stay active by posting my articles, stories, videos, gifs, memes and wanted graphics. A large number of these collectors were already somewhat familiar with me from the forums, so perhaps the greatest tool in all of social media for me was the tag. A tag is what happens when someone posts your name under a card that is for sale. Facebook will then automatically notify you. This is extremely helpful, as Facebook group postings can typically move very quickly. In a matter of minutes, any post could get buried, never to be seen again.

Eventually, if someone posted a Jose Canseco card for sale, not only would one person tag me, several would. The second person to tag me would oftentimes exclaim they were bummed out they weren't the first one to do so. Many collectors would tell me it was their goal to find a card for me that I did not yet have! I realized that not only was a large population of the collecting community looking out for me; they were rooting for me and enjoying watching my collection grow. I can't explain how it happened or why, but I am extremely grateful that it did!

Just like the forums, things can get rowdy on Facebook as well. If you want to be a person who is worthy of others wanting to tell you about cards, then don't be a person who needlessly stirs up negative drama. Don't treat people poorly, either. It reflects poorly on you and shows you to be a sour person. Who wants to help out someone like that? Do you want to be remembered as the person who shamelessly ripped apart the poor newbie who was selling his pile of 1990 Donruss commons for $50? Or do you want people to know you as the type of person who would tactfully educate the 1990 Donruss seller?

When someone tags you, show your gratitude. Far too many times, I've seen people tag others, and not get any acknowledgment. That's like opening the door for someone and them not saying thank you. Always be courteous - trust me, it helps! I'm not only saying this just for the selfish reason of getting people to like you enough to send leads your way. No, I truly believe that our community (online and offline) as a whole could benefit from simply being kind to one another.

TOOL #4: THE BREAKERS

If you are a baseball card collector nowadays, you know what a breaker is. These guys will purchase cases and cases of material, then sell spots by player or team. For example, if someone purchases a case of 2018 Museum, they may sell the Oakland Athletics spot in the case for $40, the New York Yankees for $150, and so on. When all spots are filled (all teams have buyers), the case will be broken live via video feed. This can be done on various websites, but eventually, many of them will end up on YouTube. The owner of the Athletics spot will get all of the Oakland A's cards in the case, the Yankees owner will get all Yankees, and so forth.

I'm not going to say joining breaks will make you the best Supercollector you can be. I only joined in two of them myself. I found more success by sitting back and seeing what other people were getting. There were many days that I would sit at my desk working, with a case break playing in the background. That way, if I heard Canseco's name, I could quickly take a look to see what was pulled if I wanted to try and make an offer on it before it went to eBay.

While it sometimes seemed like trying to find a needle in a haystack, my efforts did pay off a few times. In fact, I remember listening in on countless 2016 Topps Museum breaks. I often wondered why I was doing this, as it seemed like a fool's errand. After hours of these breaks were playing in the background, I heard the breaker exclaim:

"Wow! A beautiful 1/1 bat barrel of Jose Canseco!"

My heart stopped as I quickly rewound the video to watch what had just happened. Sure enough, there it was. The first 1/1 Canseco bat barrel to ever have surfaced was staring right back at me from my monitor. Just because I saw it first though, didn't mean I would be able to get it.

Getting in contact with the buyer of someone in a break can take a lot of time, effort and finesse. Many times, the breaker will be too busy to help facilitate a deal, and they may not feel comfortable giving you their customer's contact information. The best way to go about this would be to politely reach out to the breaker with the details of the card, the link to the specific break it was pulled in, the approximate time the card was pulled in the video and the name of the buyer if you can find that information. The goal is to do anything you can to make it as easy as possible for the breaker to figure out what card you want and who to put you in touch with. This will help your chances of landing the new card tremendously.

Still, I have found some breakers simply don't want to play ball. Most likely, it is because they are too busy and there is nothing in it for them. In this case, you may want to offer them a commission if you want the card badly enough. If they are still unresponsive, you can try hunting down the buyer on your own. Sometimes, a break will have the names of the buyers on the side of the screen in the video or will call out their name if they hit something big. Pay attention to these things. Sometimes, you can find out who they are by searching the forums or Facebook. Sometimes the breaker will have a channel or a Facebook group where you can ask around as well.

Many won't go to these lengths, but I have found that it is well worth the effort if you want the card badly enough. I have spent a considerable amount of time tracking down the necessary information to get in touch with owners of cards from breaks. I have found that most breakers are very helpful, but sometimes you just have to put the work in and think outside the box to do what it takes to figure out how to find the buyer directly.

TOOL #5: THE REST OF THE INTERNET

As collectors, I think we are conditioned to go straight to eBay, social media or the forums to satisfy our cardboard cravings. The truth of the matter is that there is a whole other world of cards out there that don't even touch the main avenues where cardboard commerce typically takes place. Many collectors out there have blogs showing off what they have picked up, yet hardly anyone knows about them. Do yourself a favor, and if you have an obscure card you are looking for, use the search engines to see if anything comes up.

I specifically remember trading away a 2015 Topps Tek card numbered to 25 to make a bigger deal happen. The card had not been available for sale in a long time, so I was a little apprehensive about letting it go. I ended up making the decision to trade it away, and found the same card on someone's blog, just by googling it. In four days, I had another copy of the same card back in my collection.

TOOL #6: MY OWN WEBSITE

Since I run my own website development company, it only seemed natural for me to build my own website. I started with a free blog and eventually worked up my way to building an entire website where I could write articles, post stories, show videos and more. While I absolutely loved having a place to call my own where I could do all of this, I decided to begin making the ultimate Jose Canseco website. A place where I could show every single card that I owned and every single card that was on my want list. It took me several months from the time I decided to do so until I had finished.

I spent a significant amount of time each day scanning, titling and uploading into my website. I had a good amount of help from former Supercollector Paul and current Supercollector Jamie. Paul had an amazing website showing everything he owned, so once I bought out a large chunk of his collection, I was able to utilize a lot of his scans. Jamie is still Supercollecting and has an amazing website displaying his incredible collection as well. With his permission, I was able to utilize many of his scans for my want list, with the understanding that he would be able to do the same with my scans. Even with the help of their hard work, I still had thousands of items to scan and photograph myself.

Eventually, I decided to utilize a phone app named Cam Scanner to take a picture of each card and make them appear to be scans. This would allow me to accurately depict the rich rainbow shine of the holographic foil used on many cards. This was very important to me because as time went by, I noticed myself enjoying my collection through my website a hundred times more than I was actually physically pulling the cards out to look at them. The world's largest unique collection of Jose Canseco baseball cards would be hiding in boxes two feet next to my desk, untouched because I would typically just use my website if I wanted to look at a card.

Implementing a powerful search tool feature on my website was important to me for a number of reasons. I love using my website to search a specific card and see the entire run of all versions I had of it. Searching "1987 Topps" on my website would display all of my different blank backs, wrong backs, reprints, reissues, buybacks and more. It is so much more difficult to do physically because I would have to dig into my collection and pull them out to look at them together.

I placed my physical collection in alphabetical order by card type, so if I wanted to look at all of my refractors together, it may take 15 minutes to physically pull them from all of the various boxes so that I could look at them together for a minute. When finished, I'd have to spend 15 more minutes filing them away again. The website would allow me to virtually pull all of the cards in five seconds, and was especially great for showing all card variations together. I can't quite explain it, but as a collector, I'm sure you understand. There is just something great about looking at the same card in red, yellow, pink, green, purple, orange and blue. And gold. And black. And...

I didn't build the website just so I could merely look at my own collection, though. The main reason I did it was so I could have a searchable, visual database of my collection to determine what I had and needed at all times. The website allowed me to quickly and easily see what I needed, no matter where I was. If I found a card on eBay that I wasn't sure if I had or not, I no longer had to rely on my memory and risk missing out or buying a double. Instead, I would quickly pull up my website, do a search and buy the card if I didn't already have it. In addition to this, I eventually created a searchable database on my website with visual representations of my want list and trade bait as well.

The website was instrumental for me to share with others, too, so that way they could also search if they had something I did not. I wanted it to be as easy as possible for the entire collecting community to use if they were checking up on cards for me.

As time went on, I ended up having over 1,000 Canseco cards more than any other official checklist available, because of all the different types of errors, proofs, and prototypes I had accumulated. Perhaps one of the coolest things about the website is that it became the standard checklist for Canseco collectors around the world. Countless fellow collectors would write to me thanking me for having it online. They would also say they would spend hours just looking through my collection to document their own and get lost in reading my articles.

Many collectors have balked at the idea of having their own website. They have told me they would worry about their competition seeing what they needed, then plan their bidding accordingly. Let's face it: If you know your biggest competitor needs a card that you need as well, it automatically gives you an edge. I get that completely. I made the choice, however, to expose my collection for all to see. My thinking was this: It's better for the entire world to know what I didn't yet have than to worry about five people out there who may try to cause problems if a card I wanted was posted. Based upon my experience, having your own website can be hugely beneficial in Supercollecting and can potentially put yourself ahead of the pack.

TOOL #7: GAIN EXPOSURE

This hobby has many different avenues that can help you gain exposure, and have fun at the same time! Over the past several years, I've been featured on the Topps website and have written various articles for Sports Collectors Daily. I have been interviewed several times by Eric and Paul on Beckett Radio and co-hosted a podcast with Chris, Clint and Tamer of Freedom Cardboard.

I've written for Houdini at Blowout Cards and even got my own "smilie" icon on the Blowout forums website. (If you don't know what this is, go to their website forum, create a post and click the smilies list - you'll see me there!) I've done a couple video interviews with Patrick of Radicards and was also interviewed by Shawn & Lou from The Hall of Very Good.

You can gain a lot of exposure like this, too! All you have to do is seek out opportunities and plug in. Using the tools I have described, you can work toward making your name synonymous with your collecting niche and build an army of people looking out for you as well.

Acquisition of a Lifetime

Did You Know?

Donruss and Fleer initially included sticks of bubble gum in their packs, just like Topps did. Since Topps had sole rights to do this, Donruss started packaging their cards with puzzle pieces, while Fleer switched to stickers.

I've heard people say if you were to look up the term Supercollector in the Dictionary, my face would be there. One day, I decided to search for the term "Supercollector" in Google images, and found that I was the first person to show up!

In spite of what many have probably thought, I'm not the type of guy to build a man cave and decorate it wall to wall with posters, nor do I wear Jose Canseco pajamas. I'm not knocking people that do, so if you are like Wade Boggs Supercollector Richard and have an extremely impressive man cave devoted to your favorite player, more power to you! I enjoy seeing things like this. For me personally, I've always just been about the cardboard.

When you think of a Supercollector, you may think that they are feature-worthy in one of those hoarding or obsessed television shows. For me, I kept my collecting life and "real" life completely separate. If you know me online, you know me for my custom cards, stories, gifs, memes, collection, articles, and website. A large amount of the content I created was focused on getting rare Jose Canseco cards into my collection. If you judged me based on my online persona, you might have a very difficult time picking me out of a crowd in real life based upon my lifestyle.

If you could eavesdrop in on any conversation I have with anyone in real life, baseball cards would seldom ever be mentioned. Sure, among friends and family, I was the token baseball card guy, but beyond that, no one really knew how hardcore I was about collecting, because I would never really bring it up. It wasn't anything I was hiding, though. It just never came up in conversation. Regardless, it felt like I was leading a double life. While it wasn't something I spoke about in real life, my alter-ego was always one tap away, on my phone in my pocket.

Because of my business, I spent a large amount of time online, so it was so easy to hop on over to eBay and check if there was a card I needed, or a forum to see what other collectors were saying. Since my hobbies were so baseball card-centric, my free time outside of my family would be online as well, so I was able to indulge my card collecting interests frequently throughout the day and night.

NOW, WHAT?

Over the past several years, it always seemed like I was either starting to write a story, finishing a project, making a massive deal or hot on the trail of a killer card to add to my collection. Whenever I just finished something, Canseco Supercollector AJ would always ask me the same question: *"Now, what?"*

I am not sure if there was ever a time when nothing was in the works, as I'd always have something going on that I was engrossed in. After a while though, I started wondering to myself what the next big move for my collection could be. With over 5,000 items and countless people coming to me with leads or offers on other cards daily, I was sitting pretty.

While I was thrilled to get desirable cards into my collection frequently, I couldn't help but notice that it almost got to be like an old hat. Here I was, getting rare '90s inserts, knobs, barrels, buttons, patches and all kinds of other various 1/1 cards and it just felt routine. I never got bored of them, but once they were filed away, the specialness of these landmark cards would be lost in an ocean of epic cardboard. The peak of my excitement would be the moment an actual deal was made. The level of excitement would wane from the time the card was in my hand, as it would soon become just another incredible card in my 5,000+ item collection.

With the help of what seemed to be the entire collecting community backing me, and a tsunami of new cards being released monthly, I wondered what the next big thing I could do for my collection was. It wasn't long before I started asking myself *"Now what?"*

THE $85,000 DEAL

As a Supercollector, you are always looking for the next "high". At this point in my collecting career, I felt like I had nothing else big to accomplish. Sure, I had a small number of super rare cards out there that I could still obtain, but most of them would likely take years to surface if they ever did.

For me, collecting turned into waiting to see what Canseco cards would be in upcoming releases, which seemed like a strange way to collect. It almost felt like being on an endless treadmill, trying to grab everything as they were being released. Averaged out, 2018 saw more than one new baseball card release per week throughout the entire year! Though Canseco wasn't in all of them, there have still been far more checklisted Canseco cards released in 2018 than any year before.

Years ago, AJ and I had joked about me buying him out, but would always come to the conclusion that it would simply cost too much. The more time went by, the less likely it would be as he would continually put money into his collection – with the majority of that money being put toward cards that would be duplicates for me.

After realizing that I had nothing else big to accomplish as a Canseco Supercollector, I brought up the subject of buying him out again. AJ has spent a decade meticulously putting together a world-class Canseco collection far before I started. I have spent years drooling over cards he had that I knew I would never be able to touch simply because he would never part with them. Over the years, we have gone from collecting competitors to frenemies, to friends. In my eyes, AJ's collection was by far the best out of all my competitors. This is no small feat either because there are some amazing Canseco collections out there.

I cannot stress how incredible buying his collection would be to me. Simply put, this hobby could not offer me anything better. Think about all of the vintage finds over the past several years that have made headlines in the news. You know the kind – the finds where a guy finds a bunch of beautiful tobacco cards worth tons of money while rehabbing a house. Or Mr. Mint's purchase of all those beautiful 1952 Topps cards.

To me, this was my epic find, and it wouldn't be any more exciting to me than if they were all tobacco cards. I want to be clear here with what I'm saying: Rare Jose Canseco cards meant so much more to me than any Babe Ruth bat knob, or Ty Cobb cut auto ever could. This to me, would be the deal of a lifetime. It is important to note that AJ never intended to sell his collection. He just felt that based upon my position, it made sense to move them to me.

After a while, our talks became serious, but they came with some heavy stipulations. AJ said that he would only consider selling out if I purchased everything, and at the cost of what he had paid over the years, making it a grand total of $85,000. For anyone who is heavily collecting anything for fun, that is the dream: to get back what you put into your collection whenever the time comes to sell. Unless you are intentionally purchasing for investment purposes, the odds of coming out on the other end of such a collection without any money lost are slim to none. It simply doesn't happen. But then again, people don't typically collect to make money. They collect for enjoyment.

After spending countless hours poring over his collection, I tried hard to make it all work while still being financially smart about it all. Knowing that I would have to pay every dime he paid for each card, I would breathe a sigh of relief when I would see a $300 1/1 he paid $150 for. I would also grit my teeth every time I came across a $40 card he paid $80 for because he liked the autograph so much.

Confessions of a Baseball Card Addict

I would attack it from a resale value angle to see how much of that I could recoup if I wanted to sell at some point. One thing was for sure: If we did this deal, I was going to be busy for a very long time selling off the doubles. Out of his entire collection, he had about 200 cards I did not have, so that would mean that I would have thousands of cards to sell off, for thousands and thousands of dollars.

Throughout the next few weeks, I came to the realization that no matter how hard I tried, I would not be able to get all my money back if I ever decided to sell. Then I thought about all the brand new cars that people buy for their enjoyment. They spend money each month on those and will never get their money back out of them, so why can't it be the same for cards - or at least for this monumental acquisition? That was my justification, anyway.

DEAL OR NO DEAL

When the time came to decide to go forward with this, AJ gave me a call to discuss. Through a choked up, shaky voice, he told me he couldn't sell. He was very emotional, and I could hear honest to goodness real tears through the phone. This should tell you how passionate he is about his collection. His love and passion caused him to turn down a full price offer of every single penny he had ever spent! Let that sink in for a minute. $85,000 and he turned it down. I was shocked, but understood. As a last ditch effort, I told him I would consider letting him keep the Superfractor I had purchased on eBay when we were on the phone making a deal. While that didn't stick initially, it was the catalyst for what was to come.

A couple of months down the road, AJ brought up the subject of me buying him out again, but allowing him to keep the Superfractor. He once told me that if his house was on fire and he could only grab one card to save, that would be it. I could probably count at least twenty cards I like in his collection more than that one, so my offer seemed to make sense for both of us.

Even still, it took a couple of weeks to warm up to the idea of buying him out again. Once he turned me down, I worked hard to mentally sever all ties to the fantasy that was buying him out.

After a while, I was back to where I was initially. I was white hot about making a deal, though we decided to do things a little differently. Over the next month or so, we worked closely together to take a few key cards out that I didn't care for as much as he did. After going back and forth, we agreed to a final price of $75,000 while taking out a small stack of cards that didn't mean much to me but meant a lot to him.

I cannot describe how much thought I put into this whole thing. This would undoubtedly be my largest single acquisition ever made for my collection. During this several month exercise, I would get lost in the thought of how everything would happen.

How would it all feel? Flying out to pick up the collection. Adding 80 1/1s to give me a total of 300 1/1s. To be honest, the whole ordeal kept me up many nights just dreaming about it. I would think about how cool it would be to populate my website with all the new additions and knock off all the other cards from my want list. I thought about how fun it would be to integrate the new cards into my existing collection, displaying all the bat barrels and patches together.

This acquisition meant so much more to me than just getting the cards, though. I was also excited about being able to share the news with the hobby community online. I cannot tell you how excited I was to document everything in pictures and write up an article about the entire experience. It would be pure, unadulterated joy.

One other thing I was really excited about was that I would finally have a legitimate reason to finish writing the book you are holding right now. I've wanted to write a book for years but never felt I had a good enough reason to. When my family got to hang out with Canseco at his house, I thought that might be a good final chapter, but it didn't seem quite right to finish up that way. I felt that such an acquisition as this would be the perfect ending to my book.

But God had other plans.

Doing a 180

Did You Know?

1991 Stadium Club was the first borderless baseball card to be issued by a major card company.

"Many are the plans in the mind of a man, but it is the purpose of the Lord that will stand."

- Proverbs 19:21

As I was upstairs on my computer making arrangements to purchase an airplane ticket to fly out and make the largest single acquisition for my Canseco collection ever, I decided to go downstairs and talk it over with Holly one last time. We had discussed this purchase several times over the previous few months, but I wanted to talk to her one last time before going forward with it all. I'm a firm believer that you cannot go into something this huge if your spouse is against you doing so.

The discussion with her went similarly to the previous conversations we had. She was not feeling the love for the collection like I was, but said if I was praying about it and felt God was okay with it, then she was okay. The stars were aligned, and the doors were all opened. The problem? I had this nagging feeling that something wasn't quite right. Like something was tugging on my conscience to pay attention to the still small voice. I may have heard it before regarding this subject, but perhaps I just wasn't ready to listen … or didn't want to. A month or so prior to this, I had even gone as far as making a list of pros and cons of stopping collecting. The pros outweighed the cons by a long shot, but if I'm being honest, I think my obsession just blinded me.

I can't quite explain it, but sitting in my living room with Holly that night, I felt like going through with the one thing that I wanted most would be a selfish endeavor. Just like that, I had an overwhelming sense that purchasing the collection was not what God wanted me to do. Many have told me that God doesn't care about baseball cards. Let me assure you of something. If it takes your eyes off of Him, He absolutely does care about baseball cards.

In a matter of moments, I went from looking at plane tickets to telling Holly I no longer felt right about making the purchase. With my mind going a mile a minute, I started thinking to myself if I'm not buying this collection, then what am I still doing collecting? There is nothing else left for me to accomplish. Almost in the same breath, I said words that I would never have dreamed would come out of my mouth.

"Maybe I should just go ahead and sell my collection as well."

Did I just say that out loud? What was I thinking? Years of dedication, and just like that, gone? How can I go from one extreme to another within minutes? Holly looked shocked and then smirked.

"I'm not going to tell you what to do either way – you do what you feel God is leading you to do."

Just like that, on the evening of June 8th, 2018, I made the decision to walk away from the thing that I had been passionate about for so long.

REASSURANCE FROM GOD

I contemplated quitting collecting a number of times over my collecting "career". I always wondered what it would feel like. Would I be letting people down? Would they be disappointed in me? What regrets would I have? Haven't I passed the point of no return? How hard would it be to sell everything? I then realized that it wasn't hard at all. Deciding to quit wasn't a long, arduous road. Quitting happened once I decided to do so.

Throughout all of Saturday, I felt a huge amount of peace like I hadn't felt in a long time. I didn't feel the compulsion to check my phone every 2 minutes and check eBay. I didn't have any deals going, nor did I feel compelled to stay on top of social media. It was like a huge weight had been lifted off my shoulders that I didn't know was there to begin with. It was at that moment that I felt like I had been running a marathon and was finally able to stop. The strange thing was that it never felt like a burden while I was collecting until I had stopped. I was just having fun.

Sunday, however, was a different story. I had a horrible feeling about it all that morning. I asked God to give me clear direction on what to do because I considered slipping back into it all again. Later that morning, we went to church, and I found myself sitting in the pew listening intently to what Pastor John had to say. Late into the message, his words hit me like a ton of bricks:

"Collectors...[because] we're really good in our society about being collectors. Collectors: Depending upon what you collect - how rabid you are about it, how much it costs. It may be inappropriate."

He went on to talk about a guy who collected sleigh bells, but didn't own a sleigh or a horse. He would spend thousands of dollars and travel all over the world looking for more sleigh bells. To say this sermon was applicable to me would be an understatement! He went on to ask the congregation:

"Are there any collections you need to sell?"

All of this was simply too much to take in. My eyes almost popped out of my head! Snickering to ourselves after hearing that, I dug my fingers into Holly's leg as to control my laughter. I thanked God for his clear sign to me that I had made the right decision. Since I've told this to others, some have suggested that perhaps Holly asked to our pastor to say something. Rest assured, that is not the case!

On the car ride home, we told Atticus about my decision and what all had transpired. Then Holly turned to me and told me "the rest of the story".

"So, here is something I haven't told you yet. I've been praying that God shows you if you are supposed to sell your collection – even before you ever mentioned considering selling!"

It is truly amazing to me how good God is, and I am overjoyed with how it happened so I can share it with everyone else. Let this be a reminder for you as well: Always pray for your spouse!

If you are a Supercollector or aspiring to be one, you may be tracking with me when I say there is a compulsion to keep your phone on you at all times, and to check for new listings any time you get a free moment. EBay, COMC, the forums, various social media platforms, and several other websites were all places that funneled cards into my collection, so I kept a vigilant watch on all of them. The anxiety of losing a card I needed to someone else kept me alert at all times.

Documenting all of my stories, memories, and collection on my website has helped make it easier to walk away. The community's positive feedback has greatly enhanced my journey. What everyone has written to me over the years has given me a tremendous amount of joy in this chapter of my life. I can look back at my Supercollecting journey with no regrets of walking away. I have no worries that I left anything to conquer on the table, because I squeezed every drop of satisfaction and enjoyment I possibly could from my collection.

I want to make it clear that I am not condemning collecting. My addictive personality made Supercollecting an unhealthy lifestyle for me due to the amount of brain space it took. I do urge you, however, to take a moment to think long and hard about where you are in your collecting journey and where you are in life. If you feel that you have sunk into a situation you can't get out of, I encourage you to take the steps necessary to break free from the addiction. Perhaps God has brought me through this journey to help you along in your journey! I would be overjoyed to hear if my story has helped you in some way, shape, or form.

INSPIRING PEOPLE - THE WRONG WAY

Over the past few years, many people have written to me saying how I am an inspiration to them on a daily or weekly basis. This was all so very flattering, but also very disconcerting. Throughout the past few years, I've noticed an epidemic of people posting pictures online of unopened packages saying they were hiding their "epic mail days" from their wives. When I say epidemic, I mean it, too.

It was almost as if every grown man collecting baseball cards would regularly hide their collecting addiction from their spouse. I even witnessed the destruction of a marriage that was made very public on social media – it wasn't the only divorce I've heard of due to baseball cards, either. That doesn't even get into the other potential relationship issues that can happen between a husband and wife due to a "cardboard addiction".

To think that I may have had a hand in such things by inspiring people to spend beyond their means is terrifying to me. Everybody wants to make an impact in people's lives. To be called an inspiration by so many was wonderful, but I always wondered if that very inspiration was harmful. I have a tremendous amount of gratitude for everyone who has had a hand in helping me land the best Canseco cards out there, but I also harbor guilt that it may have steered people down the wrong path.

Collecting baseball cards and directing others to collect baseball cards is not my mission in life. My mission in life is to glorify God. As a Christian, I believe this takes many forms. From leading others into a relationship with Jesus to making disciples of the nations to feeding and clothing the poor, to loving and caring for your family. I have found that obsessively collecting has the potential of being the antithesis of all these things I hold so dearly. I have probably had more fun than anyone else in this hobby of ours, but I deeply regret if my passion has rubbed off negatively on anyone. As with anything in life, there is such a thing as too much of a good thing. A bowl of ice cream is a blessing. Ten bowls of ice cream is diabetes!

GOING PUBLIC

About three weeks after I decided to retire from Supercollecting and sell out, I posted an article along with a video online. I prayed a lot. I prayed that God would use my story to help others in some way. I didn't quite know what to expect after I went public, but the response was overwhelming.

Over the next few weeks, tens of thousands of people viewed my article, and hundreds of people wrote to me. Almost everyone who reached out to me was very positive. Advice varied from "Good for you" to "At least keep a couple of cards" to "Don't do it!" I'll admit, I was worried about the responses I would get. A lot of people said they were sad and shocked. Some even suggested my decision was due to financial troubles while others speculated that Holly gave me an ultimatum. I have no idea where either of these ideas came from, but nothing could be further from the truth. Anyone who says otherwise doesn't have a leg to stand on.

I was absolutely floored by how many people actually cared. I had no idea so many people were so emotionally invested into my journey! So much so that many reached out to let me know that due to my article, they were planning on completely rethinking things in life. Others told me they were battling addiction in other areas of their life and decided to take immediate action. This was not limited to collecting, either! I was so grateful to hear that my journey and story had touched people in such a way that it could mean a dramatic lifestyle change for them. A lifestyle change that could ultimately lead to a more positive future for them and their families.

The week I announced my retirement, I had another surprise. The internet collecting community was buzzing about my news. Various hobby related blogs and news outlets were reporting it, and I was a topic of discussion on many podcasts. People were requesting interviews with me, and an Emmy award-winning television sports storyteller contacted me to do a news piece on my story. While the majority of what people were saying was positive, I remember one such podcast was quite the opposite. In what seemed to be a 15-minute profanity-laced tirade, the host of the show decided to rip me to shreds.

While all of the buzz that my announcement made was incredibly fun to experience, the hard work was ahead of me: Selling the largest unique Jose Canseco baseball card collection on the planet.

How I Sold a Six-Figure Collection

Did You Know?

1997 Flair Showcase was the first card release to introduce one of one parallels.

Around the time I went public with my decision to sell, I was featured in an article that was written by a very talented and entertaining writer named Mario at Wax Heaven.

Over the years, Mario has written many positive articles discussing my collection and custom work. I've always enjoyed and appreciated what he published on the web, but he is not one to hold back when it comes to speaking his mind.

When I posted my collection for sale, Mario stated that my journey should be seen as a cautionary tale as to what happens when you don't spend your money wisely. He then went on to say that the odds of me making my money back were slimmer than Canseco being signed to a Major League Baseball team in 2019 - that no one in their right mind would put out that kind of money for my collection.

From the outside looking in, I would have agreed with him, as he articulated what many were likely thinking. On a weekly basis, I posted jaw-dropping acquisition after jaw-dropping acquisition. Though I never publicized how much I paid, it was clear that I wasn't always making budget-minded purchases. Mario's assessment was reasonable, but I was determined to prove him and everyone else who thought I was in over my head, wrong.

HOW TO SELL A SUPERCOLLECTION

I have written articles in the past about how to sell collections, but nothing like this. Selling something of this magnitude was new territory for me, but I decided to employ my methods I would always use to see how scalable they were. Detailed below is how I sold my collection. If you are considering doing so as well, may this be a road map for you.

Before starting, I decided to take a close look at my purchasing records and add up exactly how much money I had spent on my collection over the years. The total came up to be

$107,868. This is significantly more than Jose Canseco himself received as a salary for his first full year playing for the Athletics, when he was Rookie of the Year!

Though the profits I made from wheeling and dealing cards over the years covered the entire amount I spent on my collection, $107,868 is still a lot of money to have into a collection of baseball cards, especially for one player.

Regardless of how scary the number was, it was important for me to determine where I was sitting currently, so I could set my course in the right direction. When I was buying, part of me didn't want to keep records, but I've been conditioned to understand the fact that the ability to measure anything is priceless. I never had any intention to sell at any point while I was collecting, but I just knew it would be a horrible idea to make purchases blindly. If you are considering selling and have no idea how much you have into your collection, I encourage you to sit down and make an effort to at least try. It is my experience that if you can measure your efforts, progress will be significantly easier.

Running various selling scenarios was quite sobering, to say the least, but it also gave me the wake-up call I needed to hustle like crazy. If I wanted to recoup all of my money, I had to sell $1,000 worth of Jose Canseco cards to 108 people. Or $100 worth of cards to 1,080 people. Or $10 worth of cards to 10,080 people. With well under ten big time Canseco buyers, I knew I had my work cut out for me.

SELLING TO SUPERCOLLECTORS

My core group to target initially was certainly going to be the other Supercollectors, but I knew they wouldn't be the only ones I could sell to. I had to also reach aspiring Supercollectors, casual collectors and dealers who would hope to make money off of buying from me. Reaching each group required varying strategies.

Just like any of the previous collections I had attempted to sell, I set up my spreadsheet so I could record my sales and see how close I could come to breaking even. At about three weeks before I went public with my retirement announcement, I decided to tell all of the Canseco Supercollectors that I was selling out, one at a time, in order of who I had the best relationship with. Knowing their specific tastes up front helped tremendously.

I didn't desire to pit them against each other in bidding wars, nor did I intend to create a false fear among them for losing out to someone else. Each person knew they had a unique opportunity to get in on some amazing cards before anyone else. I knew that these select few Supercollectors would likely be the only ones to pay big money for the top tier cards in my collection anyway, so it worked out perfectly. I knew it was important to remember that they may be back for more later, even if they didn't buy a ton right away. The takeaway from this for anyone interested in selling is to be fair with everyone. Don't play games, and stay true to your word. Your integrity counts on it, and your future sales do, too!

As a seller, it is crucial that you are fair, honest, and as easy to deal with as possible. Remember that your buyers will have a finite amount of money, so while they may not buy everything at first, they may come back again. The goal is to have them come back to you over and over again, and that is exactly what happened. Some of the Supercollectors who hadn't spent more than a couple hundred dollars on cards all year, ended up spending thousands with me, because they kept coming back to buy more.

SELLING TO THE PUBLIC

Within three weeks, I had sold nearly $26,000 worth of cards to the Supercollectors alone. I was shocked at how much had sold in such a short amount of time, but was still over

$80,000 away from breaking even. I decided to shift my focus on the rest of the collecting community.

My next step was to let everyone else know that I was selling my collection by writing an article. The exposure I received from it helped tremendously in my quest to sell everything. It was almost like a scene that you would expect from Black Friday at Walmart.

For the next couple of weeks, I was inundated with price requests, pulling cards from my boxes, and shipping them out. Having a website that listed and pictured everything helped tremendously from a sales and organization perspective.

I'll never forget one of the first purchase requests I received. The buyer asked if a specific Canseco autographed card would come with a certificate of authenticity. I told him I did not have one, but assured him it was real. His response was very flattering:

"I'm not talking about a COA for the authenticity of the autograph. I want a COA stating that it is coming from your collection."

I couldn't believe it! Someone cared enough about my journey that they wanted a paper stating their purchase came from my collection. After him, a number of other people asked for a COA with my signature on it as well. Some requested I sign a printed copy of their favorite article I wrote in the past, while others wanted me to sign my name on a Canseco baseball card and send it to them. A few people even sent money asking me to send them a random card just so they could have a piece of my collection in theirs.

I decided to get an embosser with my caricature and website address, so I could emboss cards from my collection and send them to whoever wanted one. In exchange, my only request was for the recipient to make a $10 donation to Compassion International. This, by the way, is still an offer that is open to

Confessions of a Baseball Card Addict

anyone interested. To think that my collection could be used to help the poor and sick gives me unspeakable joy. I challenge you to think of creative ways to use your collection to help others as well!

The fact that so many people cared so much about my journey that they wanted my autograph or a piece of my collection, was as flattering as it was baffling. It is definitely an experience I won't soon forget. Through all of this craziness, it quickly became apparent to me that this was all causing about as big of a stir as my trip to Jose Canseco's house did three years prior, if not more so.

Making the transition from selling to Supercollectors, to selling to the general public required a different strategy. I recognized that Supercollectors would likely pay top dollar for the extremely rare cards I had for sale, just as I did when I purchased them. I knew that the general public, however, will likely be looking at easier to find cards, and thus would require me to be much more flexible in my pricing. If you are too rigid, it can kill sales, so if you are looking to sell, make sure you are aware of the current market and don't be afraid to sell lower than eBay - especially if you have a lot of cardboard to sell.

Be mindful that eBay will generally take 10%, so allow your buyers to benefit from buying directly from you as opposed to buying from someone on eBay. It is a good idea also to make it appealing for your buyers to purchase several cards at once. Shipping 30 cards out in one package for $500 is a lot easier than shipping 30 cards out in 30 packages for $550. Factor your time into the equation and determine if the extra effort is worth it. Is it really all that important to make $50 more to sell them one at a time? That is something you will need to ask yourself during each and every transaction. Don't be afraid to make deals!

The cold hard truth about selling cards that weren't originally intended to be an investment is that you may lose money on them, and sometimes, by a long shot. The hardest truth to swallow is when selling a card you purchased for $500, because you and someone else were slugging it out in an eBay bidding war, only to find out the person you were bidding against is no longer interested, and the next highest bidder was at $250. If you have committed yourself to selling your collection, don't let this be an excuse not to sell. Instead, let it be a lesson for buying in the future!

I remember one card in specific that I overpaid for. I was the 2nd highest bidder at about $1,500. Eventually, I ended up paying $1,600 to the winning bidder for it, which was a big mistake. When the time came to sell, I knew full well there wouldn't be a buyer for the card anywhere near that, so I ended up selling it for $1,200. Lesson learned.

If you ever find yourself in a similar situation and have a desire to purchase something for more than it is worth, take a deep breath and try hard to think rationally about it. Remember that you can't have everything, and there are always other special cards out there. Try to envision what it would be like when it comes time to sell when there aren't any other buyers out there for anywhere near what you bought for.

Within a few weeks of my announcement, I found myself having sold over $20,500 more worth of cards without the aid of eBay, putting my total sales at around $46,500. I was ecstatic about how much had sold up to this point, but was a bit nervous, because the sales died down, everyone knew I was selling out, and I still had over $61,000 left to recoup before breaking even.

GENERATING ADDITIONAL BUZZ

After the initial rush of people making purchases died down, I decided to post an eBay listing showing the remainder of my entire Canseco collection for sale. I put a hefty price tag of $80,000 for what was left and was scoffed at by some.

My eBay listing wasn't meant just to sell the rest in one shot, though I would have certainly welcomed it. It was meant to generate some additional buzz, so my collection could have more exposure. The eye-popping eBay listing worked as intended, and people previously unknown to me started reaching out. Dealers and collectors alike contacted me, purchasing around $10,500 more worth of my cards.

A few dealers even entered serious talks with me about purchasing my entire collection. To help ensure all of the Supercollectors could get everything they wanted (and also to help my sales), I let everyone know about the potential looming buy-out, which spurned over $13,000 more in sales. At this point, I had less than $37,500 worth to sell before I broke even. It was still a lot, but with 2/3 of my funds recouped in about two months, the "game" of making my money back was more exciting than ever. I still had yet to sell anything on eBay.

SELLING ON EBAY

After following up one last time with all of my previous customers, I decided to start using eBay by listing all of my Canseco items that I could justify listing at $9.95 or more, aside from a number of 1/1s and other high-end pieces. The plan was to list several each day, so when they were automatically relisted, I would always have new listings show up on the front page every day, after the first month. In about 45 days, I was the owner of nearly a third of all Canseco baseball card listings offered at $9.95 and higher on eBay. I was very thankful for my website having scanned images of each card in my collection because it made it incredibly easy to list the cards for sale.

I wasn't too sure how well eBay would work out for me, though. I already had my entire collection for sale on my website, and surely if someone saw something they liked, they would just reach out to me. As it turned out, my eBay listings brought out even more buyers. Apparently the up-front pricing, ability to click to make an offer and concern of competition really helped sell a number of the remaining cards. It is one thing for a buyer to see a card they like on your website, and let it sit until they get around to purchasing it. It is quite another for a buyer to see it on eBay, where anyone can buy it at any moment with the click of a button.

I never posted any items for auction. They were all listed with a buy it now price and the best offer option enabled. Every card I listed was priced a bit higher than I expected them to go so that I could have the flexibility of fielding offers. Interestingly enough, out of all of the hundreds of items I sold on eBay, less than five sold at full price.

Each day, people would buy one or several items. I would follow up each buyer with a note, letting them know that I had a lot more and would be willing to make a deal with them. Sometimes, this would turn a $10 sale into a $300 sale. With each item sold, I would continue to record all transactions in my excel spreadsheet and watched with enjoyment as the total dollar amount to break even got smaller and smaller each day.

I can't quite explain it, but being fully committed to selling and having a goal to break even, made the selling process nearly as enjoyable as my collecting journey. I loved filling people's want lists, going through the sales process and listing cards. It was satisfying and enjoyable to make so many people happy with my collection.

HOME STRETCH

After a few more weeks, I found myself having sold a total of over $96,000 worth of cards. That meant I had to sell under $12,000 worth of cards to break even. I decided to get creative and post yet another listing on eBay to buy all of my Canseco eBay listings for $12,500 on October 5th, 2018. I did this because you never know who may be a buyer out there if you don't try. I'm a firm believer that you have to try big things if you want to get big results. Good things happened when I posted the rest of my collection for sale for $80,000 a couple months before, so why not give it a shot?

To be fair, I must also mention that I made several other listings along the way that never worked out. I certainly didn't find success in everything I tried, but I learned that you need to keep trying things until you find something that sticks. Each failed attempt also gave me another reason to post about my cards on social media, which meant more eyes on my collection.

The same day I posted the $12,500 listing, Canseco Supercollector Curtis reached out to me. He mentioned he wanted only cards and wanted the various other high-end cards that I had not yet listed on eBay. I quoted him a price of $14,000 and he told me that he would review everything, then get back to me.

The next morning, he texted me and said he would take them. A few hours later as I was sitting at Atticus' robotics team demo in the mall, I received notification that $14,000 had made its way to my account. A feeling of accomplishment came over me as this money represented the completion of my goal. Not only had I done the seemingly impossible by breaking even; I also turned a profit, and even had several items left to sell. It was also great to know that I had even more experience to help out others who may be in my situation. The selling tactics that I had learned over the years were, in fact, scalable to this magnitude, and it all worked out beautifully. Had I simply used eBay, and only listed single items, there is no doubt in my mind that I would still be sitting here with several thousand dollars' worth of cards left to sell. Sometimes, you have to think outside the box and hustle like crazy.

ONE FINAL TWIST

Inside of four months, I went from making arrangements to purchase a $75,000 collection, to recouping every single penny of the $107,868 I had ever spent and actually making money. Plus, it gets even better.

If you recall what I had written earlier, I love making a game out of selling, which I call Cardboard Alchemy. As a results-driven person, I thrive when I have a goal to work toward. I win the game if I can make a profit, have fun and have items left over for free. Initially, I had no desire to keep much of anything aside from base cards, because frankly, I didn't expect to sell enough to justify keeping anything else. The closer I got to my end goal, the more I realized I could, in fact, justify keeping some pieces for free, so I did just that.

Selling everything made me re-evaluate what cards I truly liked, separating them from what cards I bought just because of rarity, to complete a rainbow, or because others held them in such high regard. AJ and I would talk about purchasing certain cards as a "necessary evil" to complete a certain run. As a retired Supercollector, I have a fresh new perspective on collecting.

Many of the newer cards are gorgeous, but the excessive number of parallels just don't appeal to me as much as they once did. Scrolling through eBay, it just seems like a lot of white noise now, which is a stark difference from what my mindset was not too long ago. Don't get me wrong, I think there are some fantastic cards made nowadays, but in a run of twenty different cards in a rainbow, I may only find one or two appealing, if that.

While I love many cards such as vintage, unopened wax and certain new cards, I quickly found out that my heart was with the beautiful inserts and parallels from the '90s to mid-'00s. The cards I selected to keep combine rarity with beauty. Rarity because I wanted to keep cards that were special, and seldom ever seen elsewhere. Beauty because I never wanted to get bored of looking at them. You can never get tired of looking at a diamond.

I feel like the cards of this time period are among the most beautiful cards ever made, and their magic is rarely rivaled by new releases. It is perhaps the most sacred of time periods in modern baseball card history. Cards with jumbo patches, bat knobs and barrels will continue to be produced year after year, as they should, because they are awesome cards. There is just something about a gorgeous 1998 Donruss Crusade. Though it doesn't have a signature or premium relic piece, it scratches a very noticeable itch that today's premium relic cards simply can't touch. The same goes for several others of that time period.

When the dust settled from selling out and turning a profit, I went through my "sold" database of pictures to reminisce about what cards I truly appreciated. While there were some cards that I held onto with the intention of keeping, I found that I had already sold several that I wished I had kept, so I made it my mission to track down the rare beautiful cards I wanted back.

I asked myself "if I never sold out, and the house was burning down, what stack of cards would I grab to save?" After a little bit of creativity putting together deals and a lot of hustle, I was able to recapture many of my favorite cards.

This exercise was an interesting one, and I learned a lot about my cardboard tastes after life as a Supercollector. In my hunt to get everything as a Supercollector, I found that many of the cards I truly treasured were vastly under-appreciated and lost in my collection due to my focus always being on the next rare card I was hunting down, and not what I already had.

Surprisingly enough, I found that the thrill of hunting them down again made it way more enjoyable than if I had just kept them! Because I didn't initially hold onto the cards I wanted to keep, I was able to take another exciting adventure that included the thrill of putting together deals, enjoying the anticipation of the cards coming to me in the mail and the pleasure of placing them back in my collection. This part of my collecting experience is possibly the most fun I have ever had!

An argument can be made that perhaps the act of collecting can be more enjoyable than having a collection, if that makes sense.

When all was said and done, in addition to making a nice profit, I was able to keep a near-complete run of base and insert cards, several of my favorite cards and my favorite game-used memorabilia pieces. To top it off, I also have what seems to be a lifetime worth of game-used and player-worn items that I can use to create more customs for my collection.

I do have a confession to make, though. While I am no longer a Supercollector, I do plan on picking up a few Canseco cards here and there. I no longer have anxiety of losing out on anything, and no compulsion to finish any rainbow whatsoever. It is pure joy focusing only on cards that mean something to me. Let me encourage you to do the same - focus only on what you like, and not what others say you should get, or what checklists say you need to get in order to fulfill a run. Instead, make your own checklist, as the days of being able to obtain 100% of everything for any player or team are long gone.

FINAL THOUGHTS

Cardboard runs in my veins. It has since I was a child, and there are few things in life that I am more passionate about. Through baseball cards, I have learned many life lessons. From learning how to work deals to knowing first-hand what it looks like when you let something as harmless as baseball card collecting consume you.

If you are still collecting, learn to enjoy searching for and finding special cards, no matter how little monetary value they have. It has been my experience that the greatest joy in this hobby can oftentimes come from the anticipation of waiting for a card to come in. Don't just aimlessly throw money at cards you don't care about. Imagine having a collection where each and every card you own means something to you!

If you are planning on thinning out or selling your collection and need guidance on how to do so, it is my sincerest hope that the techniques I have documented in this book will be beneficial for you in your own journey of becoming a Cardboard Alchemist.

Now that I have seen both sides of the fence of Supercollecting, I will let you in on a little secret. The amount of enjoyment you derive from your collection is not commensurate to its monetary value. As a retired Supercollector who just a few short months ago had the world's largest unique Jose Canseco baseball card collection, I can tell you that I'm just as satisfied with the small number of cards I decided to keep as I was when I had it all. When you can learn to be content and thankful for what you have, you have truly won the game. Perhaps that is the most important of all the confessions of a baseball card addict.

Made in the USA
Middletown, DE
30 December 2018